Ms. Kathryn Holton
8957 Wynne St
Reno, NV 89506-5960

"*Clothed with Power* takes the reverence and relevance of the Old Testament and marries it to the New Testament. In a brilliant unveiling of the priestly garments, Jennifer illustrates the role of the Holy Spirit in our lives and how He clothes us with power from on high. With all its splendor, each priestly garment had significance—the same significance God uses today to spill passion and purpose over our lives."

— GARI MEACHAM, best-selling author of *Spirit Hunger* and founder of Truly Fed Ministries.

"Oh, the irony of sending a book about being 'clothed' to someone who loves to shop for clothes. But Jennifer Kennedy Dean does not take us shopping through the Scriptures to find material that will fade or become a midnight snack for moths. Instead, she digs deeply—but understandably—into what it means to be clothed with power, as Jesus promised we would be. Could be. This study will show you how. And you won't need a credit card to purchase. Joy! Joy! I love this book!"

— EVA MARIE EVERSON, director, Florida Christian Writers Conference

OTHER NEW HOPE BOOKS
BY JENNIFER KENNEDY DEAN

Power in the Name of Jesus

Power in the Blood of Christ

Live a Praying Life! Open Your Life to God's Power and Provision

Live a Praying Life: Open Your Life to God's Power and Provision
Bible Study — *Tenth Anniversary Edition*

Live a Praying Life: Open Your Life to God's Power and Provision
DVD Leader Kit — *Tenth Anniversary Edition*

Live a Praying Life: A Daily Look at God's Power and Provision Journal

Altar'd: Experience the Power of Resurrection

Life Unhindered! Five Keys to Walking in Freedom

Secrets Jesus Shared: Kingdom Insights Revealed Through the Parables

Secrets Jesus Shared DVD Kit: Kingdom Insights Revealed
Through the Parables

The Power of Small: Think Small to Live Large

Pursuing the Christ: Prayers for Christmastime

Heart's Cry: Principles of Prayer

CLOTHED WITH POWER

JENNIFER KENNEDY DEAN

CLOTHED WITH POWER

NEW HOPE
PUBLISHERS
Gospel-Centered. Missions-Driven.

BIRMINGHAM, ALABAMA

New Hope® Publishers
P. O. Box 12065
Birmingham, AL 35202-2065
NewHopeDigital.com
New Hope Publishers is a division of WMU®.

© 2013 by Jennifer Kennedy Dean
All rights reserved. First printing 2013.
Printed in the United States of America.

No part of this publication may be reproduced, stored in a retrieval system, or transmitted in any form or by any means — electronic, mechanical, photocopying, recording, or otherwise — without the prior written permission of the publisher.

Used by permission: High Priest graphic. Copyrighted material, Rose Publishing, Inc./Aspire Press.

Library of Congress Control Number: 2013941183

All Scripture quotations, unless otherwise indicated, are taken from the HOLY BIBLE, NEW INTERNATIONAL VERSION®. NIV®. Copyright ©1973, 1978, 1984, 2011 Biblica.. Used by permission. All rights reserved worldwide.

Scripture quotations marked (ESV) are from The Holy Bible, English Standard Version, copyright © 2001 by Crossway Bibles, a division of Good News Publishers. Used by permission. All rights reserved.

Scripture quotations marked (KJV) are taken from The Holy Bible, King James Version.

Scripture quotations marked (NASB) are taken from the New American Standard Bible®, Copyright © 1960, 1962, 1963, 1968, 1971, 1972, 1973, 1975, 1977, 1995 by The Lockman Foundation. Used by permission.

ISBN-10: 1-59669-373-8
ISBN-13: 978-1-59669-373-9

Cover designer: Michel Lê
Interior designer: Glynese Northam

N134114 • 0713 • 4M1

TABLE OF CONTENTS

Using *Clothed with Power* in Your Group

INTRODUCTION

I love the Old Testament. It is the Scripture Jesus used. When He taught and preached, He wasn't making up new truth. He was expositing the Scripture. His phrases and metaphors came from being steeped in Scripture. He didn't feel the need to break new ground. He brought light and understanding from the eternal Word of God, the Holy Scriptures — that which you and I refer to as the Old Testament.

The New Testament portion of our Bibles was written by men who were teaching the Old Testament Scriptures and showing the riches stored in the secret places of the Word. They had marinated in the Scripture from their earliest childhood and did not feel their Scripture to be incomplete or in need of some added material. They thought and taught and preached from the Old Testament.

I believe our New Testament to be the inspired Word of God. I believe it to have the same authority as the Word of God that the Old Testament has. Don't get me wrong. I think, though, that many of us have considered the Old Testament to be some outdated document that has little meaning in our lives.

Instead, our Old Testament is the ground of the New Testament. The New Testament is commentary on the Old Testament. When we try to separate the two, we rob ourselves of some of the wealth and beauty of the whole Word of God.

Some believe that the Holy Spirit is a promise of New Testament origin, missing the grand eternal promise that arches across the generations from beginning to end.

I learned long ago that when God inserts detail and minutiae into the Scripture — something with which the Old Testament is replete — He is not just meeting a word count, or filling space. Those details have purpose and meaning for us. Meaning that matters.

For some years I have been fascinated with the priest's garments of the Old Testament, contemplating the ornate design and the ceremony of investiture when the first priests were clothed. This is all carefully described in Scripture. I have been asking the Lord for insight into this pageantry and grandeur.

CLOTHED WITH POWER

Keep in mind that Jesus was not making up new phrases and sayings, but rather He was pulling from His tradition and training the same way we do. When He used the phrase "clothed with power from on high" to describe the coming of the Spirit, it occurred to me that the priests were the only group that were clothed with garments of heavenly design.

True, God gave instructions about different types of clothing. But only the priests were clothed by another. Moses clothed them. Piece by piece the garments were put on the priests by Moses. They were clothed.

Each of the garments was made according to a design given by God, and made by skilled workmen who were supplied with special anointing for the task. These garments were from on high.

When the garments covered the man, he became a priest. These garments endued him with a glory and honor that was not his intrinsically. Clothed in the garments, he had power and privilege to carry out what God had assigned to him.

Everything about the garments, I came to believe, illustrates the Holy Spirit's coming into our lives and clothing us with power from on high.

Several of my fascinations merged: the role of the Holy Spirit in our lives, the way to live synced to His heart and walking in His power, and the details of the priest's garments from the Old Testament. I hope you have as much fun studying *Clothed with Power* as I had researching, ruminating, and writing.

WEEK ONE

 CLOTHED WITH POWER

"I am going to send you what my Father has promised; but stay in the city until you have been clothed with power from on high" (Luke 24:49).

"You will receive power when the Holy Spirit comes on you; and you will be my witnesses" (Acts 1:8).

"Till the Spirit is poured on us from on high,
and the desert becomes a fertile field,
and the fertile field seems like a forest" (Isaiah 32:15).

DAY I

The Holy Spirit indwelling His people has always been God's intention. The Triune God—Father, Son, Spirit—is One God, not three separate entities. "Hear, O Israel: The LORD our God, the LORD is one" (Deuteronomy 6:4). This is called the *Shema* (Hebrew for "Hear") prayer. It is the centerpiece prayer in the Jewish faith. In Mark 12:29, Jesus quotes the *Shema* and identifies it as the introduction to the most important commandment. God is One. He is the Triune God, Three who are One.

The redemption plan includes the Father, who gives His Son; the Son, who gives Himself; and the Spirit, who gives life. The plan is not complete without each. "He redeemed us in order that the blessing given to Abraham might come to the Gentiles through Christ Jesus, *so that by faith we might receive the promise of the Spirit*" (Galatians 3:14; author's emphasis). The Spirit is not a watered down shadow-version of God. He is God.

The Holy Spirit is not an afterthought. He is fully God. Where the Triune God is present and working, all three are acting and working. Three in such perfect harmony that they are One. I've often compared it to Thought (Father), Word that expresses the Thought and makes Him known (Son), and Voice that carries the Word and makes Him known (Spirit). Three acting as One.

After Jesus had died on the Cross, paying for our sins as if they were His own; after His body had been bound in grave clothes and secured by government seal in a tomb; after He had risen from the dead and had shown Himself to many of His followers for a period of 40 days; after He ascended into the heavens in the sight of 500 witnesses—then the Holy Spirit was poured out on all believers.

The outpouring of the Spirit was as much an essential component of our salvation as any of the previous events. His presence was the fulfillment of the promise made by God generations before.

In Luke 24:49, Jesus refers to the Holy Spirit as "what my Father has promised." When did the Father promise the Holy Spirit?

Read Joel 2:28-29:

Upon whom will the Lord pour out His Spirit?

What will the effect be of this outpouring?

John 7:37-39:
When Jesus says, "as Scripture has said," what constituted "Scripture" for Him? In other words, was there any such thing as what we know as the New Testament?

JESUS, THE POURER FORTH

I love imagining the scene in which Jesus shouts out His invitation to come to Him for water, coupled with the promise that the living water He will impart, will flow from within anyone who drinks at His well of salvation. I wrote about this in detail in *Power in the Name of Jesus*. Let me recap.

It is at the high point of the Feast of Weeks, or the Feast of Tabernacles. On the eighth day of the feast—when the celebration had been building to its climax—the people are gathered in the Temple courtyard for the Water Pouring Ceremony. This was a celebration marked by exuberance and joy. The Talmud says, "One who has not seen the rejoicing of the water pouring has never seen a rejoicing in his life."

It was accompanied by singing and chanting. The Levitical choir, consisting of as many as 4,000 voices, sang

"Surely God is my salvation;
  I will trust and not be afraid.
The Lord, the Lord, is my strength and my song;
  he has become my salvation.
With joy you will draw water
  from the wells of salvation" (Isaiah 12:2–3).

They chanted Jehovah's invitation from Isaiah 55:1–3.

"Come, all you who are thirsty,
  come to the waters;

and you who have no money,
  come, buy and eat!
Come, buy wine and milk
  without money and without cost.

"Why spend money on what is not bread,
  and your labor on what does not satisfy?
Listen, listen to me, and eat what is good,
  and your soul will delight in the richest of fare.

"Give ear and come to me;
  hear me, that your soul may live.
I will make an everlasting covenant with you,
  my faithful love promised to David."

The choir then sang the *Hallel,* the praise Psalms 113–118. At the appropriate moment, the people joined in the singing as they waved their branches toward the altar. They sang the words of Psalm 118:25–27.

"O Lord, save us;
  O Lord, grant us success.
Blessed is he who comes in the name of the Lord.
  From the house of the Lord we bless you.
The Lord is God,
  and he has made his light shine upon us.
With boughs in hand, join in the festal procession
  up to the horns of the altar."

As they sang, the priests, waving branches and clothed in white, marched around the altar seven times on this day.

In the midst of this charged, holy moment, Jesus — whose emotions were surely stirred with love for His people — cried out in a loud voice. Imagine how loud His voice would need to have been in such an atmosphere. The word John uses for "said in a loud voice" is a word that means "scream, screech, bellow." Jesus is watching the joy and exuberance His people are experiencing as they see physical water poured out. He is overcome with emotion. It bursts from Him. It is as though Jesus says, "Are you thirsty? I have the water! Are you thirsty? Believe in Me. Come to Me. Rivers of water will be within you! You will never thirst again."

For the Israelites, the water-pouring ceremony was symbolic of the promise to pour out the Spirit on His people. The promise found in Isaiah 44:3–4 was the basis of their hope for the day when all of God's people would be filled with His Spirit, as were the prophets of old. Not only would they be filled with the Spirit, but the Spirit would be poured out of them upon the arid world.

"For I will pour water on the thirsty land,
   and streams on the dry ground;
I will pour out my Spirit on your offspring,
   and my blessing on your descendants.
They will spring up like grass in a meadow,
   like poplar trees by flowing streams."

This was among the Scriptures that the people quoted and talked about among themselves during the feast. This was a promise they treasured. All of Jehovah's people would be prophets. The word for "prophet" is *nabi* and it means "pourer-forth." It's as though Jesus says, "Come to Me and you will be a pourer-forth."

Do you see that the promise of the Spirit poured out on all God's people was a cherished vision, hoped for and looked forward to with great joy and anticipation? We can certainly look at Jesus' words to His disciples promising the Spirit, but He was basing that promise on promises already embraced by the Jewish people for generations. When Jesus referred to the promise made by His Father, He was building on a long-awaited expectation. Like the joy of the Water Pouring Ceremony, the joyful expectancy of the promise fulfilled was building among those who heard Him proclaim the imminent coming of the blessed Holy Spirit.

THE HOLY SPIRIT, THE POURED FORTH

The imagery of water was prominent as the illustration of the Spirit in the picture language of the Old Testament. His presence is cleansing and refreshing. He can both surround you and fill you. He is fluid and moving, not stagnant. He can flow out of you. I'll avoid saying He can flow from you. He flows *from* the Father, *through* the Son, but He can flow *out of* you.

On that Pentecost after Jesus had ascended to the right hand of the Father, the Holy Spirit was poured forth on God's people. They were soaked, saturated, flooded with His presence. Plunged into the flowing current of His energy; caught up in the undertow of His movement; swept into the ocean of His power. The water imagery helped define that indefinable event.

Read these Scriptures, and beside each reference, record an insight that you think that God is using the symbol of water for, in order to communicate something about His Spirit.

Isaiah 58:11

Psalm 84:6

Psalm 1:3

Isaiah 44:2-6

Isaiah 41:17-18

A note to clarify: I believe we receive the Holy Spirit in His fullness at salvation, but learn to walk in Him more fully as we mature. He is fully ours at salvation, but we learn to be more fully His as we progress. We'll delve into this later in the study.

—⟋⟍—

In English, we use the word *baptize*, a translation from the Greek *baptizo*—to immerse or submerge. However, the word John the Baptist would have been using in John, or Jesus in Acts 1:5 was the Hebrew word *mikveh*. This was a ceremony used in many ways, but instituted when the priests were first appointed. It was the cleansing ceremony that inaugurated their priestly service.

In Jesus' day, when a person converted to the teachings of a given rabbi, that person would *mikveh* into that rabbi's teaching. Those who were being baptized by John the Baptist when Jesus' ministry opened were publicly accepting John's teaching and message about repentance.

Rabbi Maurice Lamm explains the concept of *mikveh* like this in *Becoming a Jew*:

> *Jewish tradition prescribes a profound symbol. It instructs the conversion candidate to place himself or herself in a radically different physical environment—in water rather than air. This leaves the person floating—momentarily suspended without*

breathing—substituting the usual forward moving nature and purposeful stride that characterize his or her waking movements with an aimlessness, a weightlessness, a detachment from the former environment. Individuality, passion, ego—all are submerged in the metamorphosis from the larval state of the present to a new existence.

The water of the mikveh is designed to ritually cleanse a person from deeds of the past. The convert is considered by Jewish law to be like a newborn child. By spiritually cleansing the convert, the mikveh water prepares him or her to confront God, life, and people with a fresh spirit and new eyes—it washes away the past, leaving only the future. . . .

In a sense, it is nothing short of the spiritual drama of death and rebirth cast onto the canvas of the convert's soul. Submerging into waters over her head, she enters into an environment in which she cannot breathe and cannot live for more than moments. It is the death of all that has gone before. As she emerges from the gagging waters into the clear air, she begins to breathe anew and live anew—as a baby struggling to be born.
. . .

Submerging in a pool of water for the purpose not of using the water's physical cleansing properties but expressly to symbolize a change-of-soul is a statement at once deeply spiritual and immensely compelling. No other symbolic act can so totally embrace a person as being submerged in water, which must touch and cover every lesion, every strand of hair, every birthmark. No other religious act is so freighted with meaning as this one which touches every aspect of life and proclaims a total commitment to a new

*idea and a new way of life as it swallows up the old
and gives birth to the new.*

Do you see that baptism was not an invention of John the Baptist, Jesus, or Paul, but instead was a primary ceremony in Jewish life? And that Paul did not come up with its symbolism, but only transferred the symbolism of the *mikveh* ceremony into the reality of Christ?

—⁓—

In Acts 1:5, Jesus compares being baptized with water to receiving the Holy Spirit. The submersion in water—a specific ceremony of the Jewish faith called mikveh—was a picture of being immersed in the Holy Spirit at the appointed time. How does that symbol of submersion in water show something about receiving His Spirit? How does this description of *mikveh* interpret Jesus' declaration that He would baptize with the Holy Spirit?

DAY 2

When Jesus called out the invitation to become so drenched with the Spirit that He would flow out of you, He chose the image of water to frame it.

But one image does not wholly capture Him. On the pivotal Pentecost, He came as wind and fire. Neither of these images for the Spirit were foreign to the gathered group of Jewish Messiah-followers that day. In fact, like water, these were well-known and much discussed.

Examine with me the events of the Day of Pentecost when the Holy Spirit of God came to dwell on the earth in the lives of believers. Before, He had made temporary and sporadic visitations to individuals in their circumstances. This was the day when the long-promised full-spectrum salvation was finalized and completed. Jesus died to get us into heaven; the Holy Spirit descended to get heaven into us. Jesus died to pay the penalty for sin; the Holy Spirit indwells to overcome the power of sin.

—ɱ—

Read Acts 1:1-9 and consider the following:

What is the significance of Luke's statement that he had written previously about all that Jesus *"began* to do and teach" (emphasis author's)?

What does that hint about who the Holy Spirit is and what His role is on earth? Put it in your own words as you see and understand it.

Notice how, in *Commentary Critical and Explanatory on the Whole Bible,* theologian Hermann Olshausen describes it.

> Hence the grand history of what Jesus did and taught does not conclude with His departure to the Father; but Luke now begins it in a higher strain; for all the subsequent labors of the apostles are just an exhibition of the ministry of the glorified Redeemer Himself because they were acting under His authority, and He was the principle that operated in them all.

—ɱ—

When the Holy Spirit takes up where the physically present Jesus left off, it is a seamless transition. The Spirit is exactly the same Spirit through whom the man Jesus lived and ministered while in His incarnate state, or His earthly body. Jesus began His work of redemption in a body that God had prepared for Him to inhabit on earth (Hebrews 10:5), and continues it from that time until earth's end through the bodies, or lives, of His disciples. That means through you and through me. The same Spirit who worked in and through Jesus on earth, now works through you and through me on earth.

Let's look further at the Spirit's coming on the church

Read Acts 2:1-4.

When the day of Pentecost came, they were all together in one place. Suddenly a sound like the blowing of a violent wind came from heaven and filled the whole house where they were sitting. They saw what seemed to be tongues of fire that separated and came to rest on each of them. All of them were filled with the Holy Spirit and began to speak in other tongues as the Spirit enabled them.

THE OMER

"When the day of Pentecost came, . . . "

The day of Pentecost gives us the timeline for this miraculous event. Leviticus 23:15–16 explains how the day of Pentecost is identified.

From the day after the Sabbath, the day you brought the sheaf of the wave offering [Feast of Firstfruits], count off seven full weeks. Count off fifty days up to the day after the seventh Sabbath, and then present an offering of new grain to the LORD.

The day of Pentecost is determined by the Feast of Firstfruits. Pentecost is the fiftieth day—or the day that follows seven weeks after the Sabbath included in the Passover. The Greek word translated *pentecost* means "fifty days." Slightly confusing, I know. But you will see that this timeline matters.

To recap: The Feast of Firstfruits took place on the day after the Sabbath that followed Passover. It was always on the first day of the week, since the Sabbath is the seventh day. Jesus arose from the dead on the first day of the week and "became the firstfruits of them that slept" (1 Corinthians 15:20). If Pentecost was 50 days later—seven weeks plus one day—then Pentecost also took place on the first day of the week. The timeline for every detail of Jesus' saving work was prearranged and carefully choreographed. God is a God of timing and order.

Passover	Crucifixion	Friday
Firstfruits	Resurrection	Sunday that follows Passover
Pentecost	Giving of the Spirit	Sunday 50 days later

From His resurrection to His ascension, Jesus taught on earth for 40 days. From His ascension to Pentecost, the early church was gathered in prayer for 10 days.

The Feast of Firstfruits was instituted by God to celebrate the coming harvest. On the Feast of Firstfruits, people who were in Jerusalem for

Passover journeyed to the Temple to offer a symbolic sheaf of barley, cut from their crop. This was called the *omer.* In offering the *omer,* the person was giving thanks for the harvest to come and proclaiming faith that this was but the firstfruits of a great harvest. No need to keep a grasp on this first bud because God could be counted on to bring a full, rich harvest. The *omer* stood for all that would follow. The day of Pentecost — 50 days later — was the celebration of the harvest they had reaped. It was also known as the Feast of Harvest.

Recognizing the timing of events, as Jesus faced His crucifixion in the days leading up to Passover, He called His disciples together and said: "Very truly I tell you, unless a kernel of wheat falls to the ground and dies, it remains only a single seed. But if it dies, it produces many seeds" (John 12:24). Do you see that He was looking ahead to the day just ahead when He would be the *Omer?* His resurrection would be the firstfruit of a great harvest. Jesus already knew that when the day of Pentecost came, there would be a great harvest of lives. He knew that His physical resurrection would be the firstfruit of a mass resurrection when His Holy Spirit unleashed His quickening power en masse.

"When you were dead in your transgressions and the uncircumcision of your flesh, He made you alive together with Him, having forgiven us all our transgressions, having canceled out the certificate of debt consisting of decrees against us, which was hostile to us; and He has taken it out of the way, having nailed it to the cross" (Colossians 2:13-14 NASB).

Our Jesus is our *Omer.* He first offered Himself to God as Passover Lamb, then as the *Omer* of the great harvest of what He had died to produce — like a grain of wheat that falls into the ground. On that Pentecost recorded in Acts, the fullness of the salvation for which He paid so high a price was poured out without measure.

Jesus, our Firstfruit or *Omer,* is the archetype of a new creation. When we look at Him, we see the promise for our own lives. We see the pattern for what God has for us. What we see is that He, in His earthly life, was powered by the Holy Spirit—the same Holy Spirit who came at Pentecost and who lives in us now.

"And if the Spirit of him who raised Jesus from the dead is living in you, he who raised Christ from the dead will also give life to your mortal bodies because of his Spirit who lives in you" (Romans 8:11).

—∿—

How is Jesus as the *Omer,* or Firstfruit, of your life meaningful to you today?

Looking at your *Omer,* what promise do you see for your life?

WIND AND FIRE

"Suddenly a sound like the blowing of a violent wind came from heaven . . ."

The evidences and demonstrations of the Spirit's coming started with sound. The sound of a mighty wind. People who have experienced tornadoes describe the sound that precedes the event—the sound of a rushing, violent wind. I have heard it described several times as the sound of a freight train. The sound in the room where the worshippers were gathered that day must have been reminiscent of that roaring. Loud enough to drown out any other sound and to announce the coming of the Spirit of God. It was loud enough to be heard by those not in the room. It is this sound that gathered the crowd.

"They saw what seemed to be tongues of fire that separated and came to rest on each of them" (Acts 2:3).

After hearing the roaring of wind, they saw something that looked like fire. According to scholar John Hackett, in *Word Studies in the New Testament,* and others, the meaning seems to be that "the fire-like appearance presented itself at first, as it were, in a single body, and then suddenly parted in this direction and that; so that a portion of it rested on each of those present" (Hackett).[1] This fire came to rest on each individual, yet was one single entity. The fire that rested over each head was the same fire, but individually distributed. "There is one body and one Spirit, just as you were called to one hope when you were called; one Lord, one faith, one baptism; one God and Father of all, who is over all and through all and in all" (Ephesians 4:4–6).

The Spirit filled each individual but also blended them and coalesced them into one body. The mighty work of unifying that only the Holy Spirit could do might be one of the most astonishing miraculous evidences of His coming.

THE MIRACLE OF HEARING

"All of them were filled with the Holy Spirit and began to speak in other tongues as the Spirit enabled them. Now there were staying in Jerusalem God-fearing Jews from every nation under heaven. When they heard this sound, a crowd came together in bewilderment, because each one heard their own language being spoken" (Acts 2:5–6).

If you have ever tried to communicate with a person of a different language, you know the barriers language can present. Even if you can find a way to communicate simply, it takes words to put across an idea. Even traveling from region to region in your own country, the same word may have a different meaning.

A few years ago I moved to a town in western Kentucky. Before, if a person were to say, "I don't care to go to the store," I would have heard it as, "I don't want to go to the store." Here, if someone says those same words, they mean, "I don't mind going to the store." Same words, exactly opposite meaning. Words matter. And the definition of any given word matters.

On the pivotal Pentecost day, once the attention of the crowds had been caught by the tornadic noise, the great miracle of hearing occurred. Whatever language the newly Spirit-filled believers spoke, the hearer heard it in his own language.

"Utterly amazed, they asked: "Aren't all these who are speaking Galileans? Then how is it that each of us hears them in our native language? Parthians, Medes and Elamites; residents of Mesopotamia, Judea and Cappadocia, Pontus and Asia, Phrygia and Pamphylia, Egypt and the parts of Libya near Cyrene; visitors from Rome (both Jews and converts to Judaism); Cretans and Arabs — we hear them declaring the wonders of God in our own tongues!" (Acts 2:7–11).

When the believers opened their mouths and let the Spirit "give them utterance," the Spirit worked on the other side of the equation with equally amazing power. He hand-delivered His message to each listener. Imagine the scene, as people of different cultures and tongues stood listening to the same speaker, but each hearing it in his native language. Most of these people were likely multilingual to some extent. They may have been able to pick out enough words to get the gist of a message delivered in a language other than their own. But the Holy Spirit spoke His word in each person's personal language.

This was the finalization of the New Covenant relationship that had been promised in Ezekiel 11:19–20.

"I will give them an undivided heart and put a new spirit in them; I will remove from them their heart of stone and give them a heart of flesh. Then they will follow my decrees and be careful to keep my laws. They will be my people, and I will be their God."

He is using covenant language when the promise includes the words "They will be my people and I will be their God" (Exodus 6:7). When He poured out His Spirit on His people, it was the completion and fulfillment of the promise that had its beginning generations earlier.

—⟶⟵—

Stop to think through what the Spirit is saying to you now about Himself in this passage. How is He taking the Word and hand-delivering it to you?

DAY 3

When God inaugurated His first covenant with His people at Sinai, the first evidence of His presence was sound. Rabbinical scholars consider the giving of Torah to be the first Pentecost because it occurred 50 days after the crossing of the Red Sea. The Jews arrived in the Sinai Desert in the third month on the first day, according to Exodus 19:1. A timeline is given through the account which the Rabbis calculate to be exactly 50 days from the crossing.

At the crossing, the nation of Israel was "born again." When they set foot on dry ground after passing through the Red Sea, they stood as the

Firstfruits of the chosen nation. Fifty days later God gave them Torah and brought them into a covenant relationship with Him. Pentecost is called the season of the giving of Torah *(Z'man Matan Toraseinu)* because it is the day God revealed Himself to His people at Sinai.

OPENING ACT

On that day, the people first heard sounds that emanated from the heavenly realms. "On the morning of the third day there was thunder and lightning, . . . , and a very loud trumpet blast. Everyone in the camp trembled" (Exodus 19:16). Then they saw fire. "Mount Sinai was covered with smoke, because the LORD descended on it in fire. The smoke billowed up from it like smoke from a furnace, and the whole mountain trembled violently" (Exodus 19:18). "When the people saw the thunder and lightning and heard the trumpet and saw the mountain in smoke, they trembled with fear" (Exodus 20:18).

On the day of Pentecost recorded in Acts, the people had similar experiences of the presence of God through His Holy Spirit.

GIVING OF TORAH	GIVING OF SPIRIT
Commandments on tablets of stone (Ex. 24:12	Commandments on our hearts (Jer. 31:33; 2 Cor. 3:3)
Written by finger of God (Ex. 31:18)	Written by Spirit of God (2 Cor. 3:3; Heb. 8:10)
3,000 slain (Ex. 32:1-8, 26-28)	3,000 receive eternal life (Acts 2:38-41)
Letter of Torah (Romans 2:29; 7:6; 2 Cor. 3:6)	Spirit of Torah (Romans 2:29; 7:6; 2 Cor. 3:6)

Jewish theology holds that on that first Pentecost, the people accepted God's proposal that He would be their God and they would be His people. Their obedience to His Torah would set them apart from all other nations and mark them as His.

On the pivotal Pentecost when the Spirit was poured out on God's people, He set them apart and His presence in their lives marked them as His. The presence of the Spirit in them transformed them and empowered them so radically that it attracted the attention of even casual observers.

By the days of the great Pentecost in Acts and continuing to today, the tradition of "Torah Portions" — the practice of reading and studying a set section of Torah on the Sabbath and during Feasts — was in effect. Part of the Torah Portion for Pentecost (also known as *Shavout*, or Feast of Weeks) is Exodus 19:1-20:23. On that day, the Messiah-followers saw the ancient words of covenant fulfilled.

God has poured out His Spirit on His people. His Spirit indwells each believer at the moment of salvation. It is the coming of His Spirit into a life that changes that person's state "from death to life" (1 John 3:14).

—⟋⟍—

From the following Scriptures, highlight the words and phrases that tell you that the Spirit is the seal or proof of your salvation, and that He comes to indwell you at the moment of your salvation.

"And this is how we know that he lives in us: We know it by the Spirit he gave us" (1 John 3:24).

"You, however, are not in the realm of the flesh but are in the realm of the Spirit, if indeed the Spirit of God lives in you. And if anyone does not have the Spirit of Christ, they do not belong to Christ" (Romans 8:9).

"The Spirit himself testifies with our spirit that we are God's children" (Romans 8:16).

DAY 4

Once the Spirit has come to take up residence in our lives, we become the Temple of the Holy Spirit. "Don't you know that you yourselves are God's temple and that God's Spirit dwells in your midst?" (1 Corinthians 3:16).

The Spirit who had been present with God's people always, is now present *in* God's people. The Holy Spirit is so one with Jesus that He is Jesus in spiritual form. I don't think we have to draw a distinct demarcation between the Father, Son, and Spirit. They are Three in such harmony that They are One. They are three entities. They have different functions, but different functions in the same action. Where one is present and working, so are all. He is a triune God. We don't need to parse Him.

A popular way to define the mystery of the three-in-one God is the illustration of water in its three forms: liquid, vapor, solid. I think this illustration falls short because water is not all those things at one time. God is always three Persons, yet He is always One. As we continue in this exploration of the Holy Spirit, be aware that when He is working, it is all of God working.

When Jesus specifically promised the Holy Spirit to His disciples, He blurred the lines between Himself and His Spirit. Look with me.

"And I will ask the Father, and he will give you another [Counselor] to be with you forever — the Spirit of truth. The world cannot accept him, because it neither sees him nor knows him. But you know him, for he lives with you and will be in you. I will not leave you as orphans; I will come to you. Before long, the world will not see me anymore, but you will see me. Because I live, you also will live. On that day you will realize that I am in my Father, and you are in me, and I am in you. Whoever has my commands and obeys them, he is the one who loves me. He who loves me will be loved by my Father, and I too will love him and show myself to him" (John 14:16-21).

HOLY SPIRIT	JESUS
The world neither sees Him or knows Him	In a little while, the world will not see Jesus
But you know Him	You will see Jesus; Jesus will show Himself to you
He lives with you and will be in you	Jesus will come to you; He will be in you

Jesus says that the Holy Spirit, who has been *with* them, will soon be *in* them. Jesus will return to them in the form of His Spirit and His presence that has been outside them with them, will indwell them.

Jesus promised that the Father will send "another Comforter." Like, I have a sister, and I have *another* sister. One doesn't take the place of the other. I think, based on what I have just laid out from Scripture, that Jesus says that the *Holy Spirit*, who is just exactly like Jesus, and the *Father*, who is just exactly like Jesus, and *Jesus*, who is just exactly like the Father and like the Spirit, will make *Their* home in you. Triune God, Three-in-One God, will make His home in you and will each perform His role in the Trinity. Three in such perfect harmony that they are One. "I am in my Father, and you are in me, and I am in you."

God is not trapped in time and space and not subject to the laws of location. Jesus can be at the Father's right hand in the heavenlies *and in you* at the same time. The Father can be on the universe's throne — and in you. The Spirit can be active in the heavenly realms — and in you.

Do you believe that the Holy Spirit can be active in me, and in you, and in millions of believers at one time? Do you believe that Jesus can be working in my life, and in your life, and in the lives of millions of believers at one time? That God the Father can be working in millions of situations all over the planet at the same time? Of course you do. The Eternal God is not limited to the laws of geography.

The point I want you to see is that the Scripture makes much of the reality that Jesus — in whom all the fullness of the Deity lives

(Colossians 2:9)—lives in *you. In you.* In the same conversation that is recorded in John 14, where we have just been looking, Jesus continues in the same vein as John 15 picks up. Hear what He says: "Remain in me, and I will remain in you. . . . I am the vine; you are the branches. If a man remains in me and I in him, he will bear much fruit; apart from me you can do nothing" (John 15:5; 45). And John writes later: "This is how we know that we live in him and he in us; he has given us of his Spirit" (1 John 4:13). "So that Christ may dwell in your hearts through faith" (Ephesians 3:17).

A.B. Simpson explains it like this in *Power from on High*:

> *It is Christ's province to baptize with the Holy Ghost. The sinner does not come first to the Holy Spirit, but to Christ. . . .*
>
> *Jesus received the Spirit from the Father. We receive the Spirit from Jesus. It is necessary for us, in order that we may fully receive the Holy Ghost, that we shall first receive Christ in His person as our Savior and as our indwelling life.*
>
> *The Father gave the Spirit to Him not by measure and, if He dwells in us, He will bring the Spirit with Him, and He shall dwell in us likewise in the same measure in which He dwells in Jesus. . . .*
>
> *It is the Christ within us, that still receives the Holy Ghost.*
>
> *And so, when our Master was about to leave the world, it is significantly stated that He breathed upon them, and said: "Receive ye the Holy Ghost." The Holy Spirit came upon them through the breath of Christ. This significant action emphasized the fact that the Spirit was imparted to them from His own person and as His own very life. It is true that the act of breathing on them did not bring immediately the residence of*

the Holy Ghost into their hearts, for this could not be until after the day of Pentecost. But it was meant to connect it with Himself, so that when the Holy Ghost did descend and dwell in them they would receive Him as the Spirit of Jesus, and as communicated to them by the breath and the very kiss of their departing Master.

As we have already seen, the Holy Ghost comes to us as the Spirit of Christ and even as His very heart, the One who wrought in Him His mighty works and repeats them in us.

Would we receive the baptism with the Holy Ghost, let us receive Jesus in all His fullness. Let us draw near to His inmost being, and from His lips let us in-breathe the Spirit of His mouth.

Jesus is no longer present in His physical body, but He is present through His Spirit. His presence in Spirit form in us is more effective for guiding, providing, protecting, teaching, and correcting. The very same Jesus who was and is to come, is living His (present-tense) life in you right now through His Spirit. You are His Temple, His dwelling place on the earth.

PRIESTS

We become also the priests of that Temple. The ones who serve and tend and wait on our great King, who inhabits His dwelling. The ones who minister in the name of our King. On that first Pentecost when covenant was established and Torah given, He proclaimed: "Although the whole earth is mine, you will be for me a kingdom of priests and a holy nation'" (Exodus 19:5–6). This promise and commission was spoken again through Peter.

"As you come to him, the living Stone — rejected by humans but chosen by God and precious to him — you also, like living stones, are being built

into a spiritual house to be a holy priesthood, offering spiritual sacrifices
acceptable to God through Jesus Christ" (1 Peter 2:4–5).

And John saw it in his revelation of the heavenly realms:

"You are worthy to take the scroll
and to open its seals,
because you were slain,
and with your blood you purchased for God
persons from every tribe and language and people and nation.
You have made them to be a kingdom and priests to serve our God,
and they will reign on the earth" (Revelation 5:9–10).

The theme of a priesthood of believers runs through from the giving
of Torah to the final scenes. God doesn't waste words. The intricate
descriptions of the priests' garments surely have eternal purpose and
significance.

Our salvation is so detailed and beyond comprehension that one
picture or illustration will not do. No one-dimensional line drawing can
convey the vast grace poured out on our lives. God paints a picture that
has depth and detail; that is nuanced and shaded; that is multicolored
and many-layered.

The detail in the Old Testament regarding priest's clothing is vivid
and elaborate. When Jesus described the coming of His Spirit, He called
it being clothed with power from on high. Each of the elements of the
priests' clothing represents some way in which the Holy Spirit would
clothe our lives in His power—power He brings with Him from on
high. The power with which He clothes us is heaven's very own power.
The same Spirit who empowered Jesus during His days on earth. The
same Spirit who raised Jesus from the dead. The one and only Holy
Spirit who is from the beginning and who is fully God. He covers us
and fills us. He is both with us and in us.

As we examine the priest's clothing, we will get a glimpse of the Holy Spirit in our lives. We will find that there is a covering for every part of our lives.

Consider what it means to be clothed with power. Think through that picture. Consider each part of your body and what each represents. As the Holy Spirit brings it alive for you during this study, which part of your life most needs power dressing right now? Invite the Holy Spirit to be the covering and to clothe you with Himself.

DAY 5

OUR GREAT HIGH PRIEST

As we work our way into the beautiful imagery of the priest's garments, let's put one more plank down in the ground floor. We have a great High Priest. He became High Priest through His actions as our Savior. High Priest was a designated title He did not hold before His incarnation.

"For this reason he had to be made like them, fully human in every way, in order that he might become a merciful and faithful high priest in service to God, and that he might make atonement for the sins of the people. Because he himself suffered when he was tempted, he is able to help those who are being tempted" (Hebrews 2:17-18).

As a kingdom of priests (see 1 Peter 2:4-5), we are not Jesus. Only Jesus is High Priest. But we are clothed in Him (Romans 13:14). The garments of the High Priest cover us. We are the vessels that contain

Him, and we are the lives that express Him. As we look at the details of the High Priest's garments, we will see their parallels in the role of the Holy Spirit in our lives.

Our High Priest shows us what humanity clothed in power looks like. "As He is, so also are we in this world" (1 John 4:17 KJV). "As the Father has sent Me, I also send you" (John 20:21 NASB). This statement was followed by "Receive the Holy Spirit" (John 20:22). How are we to be as He is in this world? How are we to be equipped for being sent by Jesus into the world? By receiving and living in the power of the Holy Spirit, just as our great High Priest lived in the power of the Spirit during His life as a man sent by God.

POWER IN YIELDEDNESS

One thing that astounds me about the incarnation is that the Son held heaven's highest place, equal in every way to the Father and the Spirit. He had a certain kind of glory that He relinquished in order to be our High Priest and Savior. As He was facing His crucifixion, He prayed, "Now, Father, glorify Me together with Yourself, with the *glory which I had with You before the world was*" (John 17:5 NASB; author emphasis). In *Experiencing the Spirit,* authors Henry and Mel Blackaby state it this way: "He chose to live under the limitations that come with a physical body."

In Philippians 2:6–8 we read:

"Although He existed in the form of God, did not regard equality with God a thing to be grasped, but emptied Himself, taking the form of a bond-servant, being made in the likeness of men. Being found in appearance as a man, He humbled Himself by becoming obedient to the point of death, even death on a cross" (author's emphasis).

He didn't just come disguised as a man, but He became a man. Emptied Himself. Relinquished His rightful glory and position. The Master and

Ruler voluntarily became obedient to the Father, and yielded Himself to be led and empowered by the Spirit. He did not empty Himself of His essential nature as God. That was who He was, is, and always will be. But He laid aside His independently acting power and authority and became obedient.

He was the prototype of a fully human, albeit perfect, man living in complete dependence on the Spirit and in absolute obedience to the Father. By essential nature, still fully God, Jesus limited His nature to a man's frame—body and soul—and so demonstrated the eternal plan for humanity.

Because He yielded Himself in every way to the Spirit's leading to be the vehicle for the Father's work, Jesus exuded power. As we will see in the details for the priests' garments, He showed how a life permeated with the power of the Spirit spilled over as rivers of living water to those around Him. Every area of His humanity was a conduit for the power of the indwelling Spirit. All the power that flowed *from* Him is power that was flowing *through* Him from the Spirit who dwelled *in* Him.

—⟋⟍—

From the following statements, identify the source of Jesus' power.

Jesus, full of the Holy Spirit, returned from the Jordan and was led by the Spirit in the desert (Luke 4:1).

Jesus returned to Galilee in the power of the Spirit, and news about him spread through the whole countryside (Luke 4:14).

The scroll of the prophet Isaiah was handed to him. Unrolling it, he found the place where it is written: "The Spirit of the Lord is on me, because he has anointed me to preach good news to the poor. He has sent me to proclaim freedom for the prisoners and recovery of sight for the blind, to release the oppressed" (Luke 4:17–18).

At that time Jesus, full of joy through the Holy Spirit, said, "I praise you, Father, Lord of heaven and earth, because you have hidden these things from the wise and learned, and revealed them to little children. Yes, Father, for this is what you were pleased to do" (Luke 10:21).

You know what has happened throughout Judea, beginning in Galilee after the baptism that John preached—how God anointed Jesus of Nazareth with the Holy Spirit and power, and how he went around doing good and healing all who were under the power of the devil, because God was with him (Acts 10:37–38).

From the following statements, identify to whom Jesus was obedient.

"Jesus gave them this answer: 'I tell you the truth, the Son can do nothing by himself; he can do only what he sees his Father doing, because whatever the Father does the Son also does. For the Father loves the Son and shows him all he does'" (John 5:19–20).

"For the very work that the Father has given me to finish, and which I am doing, testifies that the Father has sent me" (John 5:36).

"I do nothing on my own but speak just what the Father has taught me. The one who sent me is with me; he has not left me alone, for I always do what pleases him" (John 8:28–29).

"Jesus replied, 'If I glorify myself, my glory means nothing. My Father, whom you claim as your God, is the one who glorifies me'" (John 8:54).

"The reason my Father loves me is that I lay down my life— only to take it up again. No one takes it from me, but I lay it down of my own accord. I have authority to lay it down and authority to take it up again. This command I received from my Father" (John 10:17–18).

"For I did not speak of my own accord, but the Father who sent me commanded me what to say and how to say it. I know that his command leads to eternal life. So whatever I say is just what the Father has told me to say" (John 12:49–50).

"The words I say to you are not just my own. Rather, it is the Father, living in me, who is doing his work" (John 14:10).

"These words you hear are not my own; they belong to the Father who sent me" (John 14:24)

"The world must learn that I love the Father and that I do exactly what my Father has commanded me" (John 14:31).

—◆—

Jesus lived out obedience to the Father that was empowered by the Spirit. This is what we are to do: Obey the Father in the same way that Jesus obeyed the Father (John 15:10). By the indwelling power of His Holy Spirit. Our lives must be clothed with His power.

WEEK TWO

CLOTHED WITH DIGNITY AND HONOR

"Make sacred garments for your brother Aaron to give him dignity and honor. Tell all the skilled workers to whom I have given wisdom in such matters that they are to make garments for Aaron, for his consecration, so he may serve me as priest. These are the garments they are to make: a breastpiece, an ephod, a robe, a woven tunic, a turban and a sash. They are to make these sacred garments for your brother Aaron and his sons, so they may serve me as priests. Have them use gold, and blue, purple and scarlet yarn, and fine linen" (Exodus 28:2–5).

DAY I

The carefully prescribed priests' garments imparted to the priests dignity and honor they did not inherently possess — dignity and honor that was not their own. Only when they were wearing these garments were they endued with dignity and honor. These words are also translated "glory and beauty" (NASB, NKJV, HCSB, and others).

The Hebrew words translated here "dignity" and in other places "beauty," is from the verb *pāar*. According to *Theological Wordbook of the Old Testament*, the subject of the verb is always God and the recipient is His children. God does the beautifying. The beauty the garments bring is derived from God, not inherent in the clothing itself.

The Hebrew word translated "honor" or "glory" is the word *kābôd*. The rabbis coined the word *Shekina* to stand for the glory of God. This is not a word found in Scripture, but is prevalent in Hebrew texts to stand for the concept of glory. Shekina Glory is defined as *the visible manifestation of the presence of Jehovah God* — often showing up in the form of a cloud, light, fire, or combinations of these. It is the majestic presence or manifestation of God in which He descends from heaven to *dwell (shakan)* among men.

So, *glory* can mean the visible presence. God's presence was made visible, for example, in the cloud of glory that rested over the tabernacle, or filled the sanctuary. To complete the meaning of *glory* as "weightiness" or "worthiness," when God reveals Himself, His holiness and worthiness are evident. That which glorifies God is that which reveals His character and manifests Him in visible ways. The priests' garments were to be a visible symbol of God's invisible presence. They were to define Him and reveal Him to His people.

The symbol of the priests' garments as a visible representation of God's presence points us to the reality that when we are clothed with power from on high—the Holy Spirit—our lives become the living testimony to the Spirit, who testifies of Jesus, who testifies of the Father.

Being clothed with power makes us the evidence and convincing proof of the living, present, powerful Jesus. He dresses us in Himself and beautifies our lives, giving us a beauty and a glory that we do not possess apart from Him.

"Remain in me, as I also remain in you. No branch can bear fruit by itself; it must remain in the vine. Neither can you bear fruit unless you remain in me. I am the vine; you are the branches. If you remain in me and I in you, you will bear much fruit; apart from me you can do nothing" (John 15:4–5)

In the symbol of the high priests' garments, we see this clearly. The garments covered them—covered their sinfulness so that they could enter the holy dwelling of the holy God. They could not enter the Tabernacle or perform priestly duties if not fully dressed in their garments. They could not wear the holy garments outside the tabernacle. The garments fitted them for their service to God. The Talmud states: "While they are clothed in the priestly garments, they are clothed in the priesthood; but when they are not wearing the garments, the priesthood is not upon them" (BT Zevachim 17:B).

"Once the priests enter the holy precincts, they are not to go into the outer court until they leave behind the garments in which they minister, for these are holy. They are to put on other clothes before they go near the places that are for the people" (Ezekiel 42:14).

"Aaron and his sons must wear them whenever they enter the tent of meeting or approach the altar to minister in the Holy Place, so that they will not incur guilt and die" (Exodus 28:43).

God is always ready to provide a covering for us so that we can be in His presence. From Adam and Eve in the Garden of Eden, to believers now who are covered by the blood of the Lamb and clothed with power from on high.

—⟋⟍—

Since you have received Christ as Savior and so have His Holy Spirit in residence, what has changed about your character or personality?

What are you able to do or be that you could not do or be apart from Him?

What evidence of the Spirit do you see in your life?

DAY 2

The priests' garments and the Tabernacle are all part of a single setting for worship and obedience in the things of God. The materials of the Tabernacle are repeated in the design of the priests' garments. The instructions are to make the garments for Aaron (the first High Priest) "for his consecration, so he may serve me as priest" (Exodus 28:3). The service of the priesthood was carried out within the confines of the Tabernacle.

We find colors, fabrics, and metals consistent in both Tabernacle and priests' garments. Among those who have studied and written on these as types, there is little debate about what each of these elements represents. Among scholars on the topic there is nearly unanimous agreement on the typology.

COLORS

Blue

The blue is a bright sapphire blue, the color of *lapis lazuli*. This color is described in heavenly visions as the color of the crystal sea surrounding the throne and of the throne itself.

Moses and Aaron, Nadab and Abihu, and the seventy elders of Israel went up and saw the God of Israel. Under his feet was something like a pavement made of lapis lazuli, as bright blue as the sky" (Exodus 24:9–10).

Above the vault over their heads was what looked like a throne of lapis lazuli, and high above on the throne was a figure like that of a man (Ezekiel 1:29).

This skyblue dye, or sapphire blue, resembled the brilliant color of indigo blue. This dye was extracted from the secretions of the murex snail, murex trunculus, found on the eastern coast of the Mediterranean Sea.

This blue was also in the fabric that draped the ceiling of the Tabernacle. Blue is considered the color that represents the heavenly realm, or the spiritual eternal realm.

Crimson or Scarlet

The Hebrew word translated "scarlet" or "crimson" is *tôleâ* and it means "worm," referring to a very specific worm from which the deep-red dye was extracted. This worm gives a very detailed picture of the blood shed for us from the earthly body of our Savior. This is the same word translated "worm" in Psalm 22:6, a messianic psalm, in which Messiah says these words: "I am a worm and not a man." I think this definition will help you understand that statement. Henry M. Morris, in his book *The Biblical Basis for Modern Science*, explains this:

> When the female of the scarlet worm species was ready to give birth to her young, she would attach her body to the trunk of a tree, fixing herself so firmly and permanently that she would never leave again. The eggs deposited beneath her body were thus protected until the larvae were hatched and able to enter their own life cycle. As the mother died, the crimson fluid stained her body and the surrounding wood. From the dead bodies of such female scarlet worms, the commercial scarlet dyes of antiquity were extracted. What a picture this gives of Christ, dying on the tree, shedding His precious blood that He might "bring many sons unto glory" (Hebrews 2:10).

The Hebrew word *ādām* translated Adam or mankind comes from the Hebrew word *ădāmâ*, which is translated "ground" or "dirt" but literally means "red." God created *ādām* (man) from the *ădāmâ*, dust).

Red—crimson, scarlet—is the color of man, and specifically of the humanity of Jesus.

Purple

Red (Jesus' humanity) and blue (heavenly nature) are two opposite ends of the color spectrum. When those two colors combine, they make purple. It is the representation of the eternal Son who took upon Himself the form of a man in order to secure our salvation, and bring many sons to glory (Hebrews 2:10).

As His humanity and His divinity blended, He became the mediator between God and mankind. The role of the High Priest is to be a mediator. He represents mankind to God, and God to mankind. Mediator. "For there is one God and one mediator between God and mankind, the man Christ Jesus" (1 Timothy 2:5).

He was always God. He was always the Son. But He became a High Priest. "For this reason he had to be made like them, fully human in every way, in order that he might become a merciful and faithful high priest" (Hebrews 2:17). A mediator has to be identified with both parties.

White

White is the color of purity and holiness.

"Though your sins are like scarlet,
they shall be as white as snow;
though they are red as crimson,
they shall be like wool" (Isaiah 1:18).

"Cleanse me with hyssop, and I will be clean;
wash me, and I will be whiter than snow" (Psalm 51:7).

In Jesus, the purity and holiness are His inherent nature. In us, it is the holiness and purity of Jesus covering us and imparted to us by His Spirit.

COLOR-CODED

Each color tells a portion of the great salvation story. The color themes in the Tabernacle are repeated in the priests' garments. It is all one experience. The One who is doing the sanctifying and the ones who are being sanctified are all parts of a whole. Could it be that the Triune God is represented here in their roles?

The Father is the one being served *(Shekinah Glory)*. *"So they may serve me as priests"* (Exodus 28:1).

The Son is the setting in which that service happens (Tabernacle). "For in him we live and move and have our being" (Acts 17:28).

The Holy Spirit is carrying out the activity of service (priests). "For it is we who are the circumcision, we who serve God by his Spirit" (Philippians 3:3).

God is telling a panoramic, epic story. He engages all our senses as He portrays the fullness of our salvation. We can see the pageantry, hear the cacophony, smell the pungent odors. And He puts us at the apex of this drama. Without the priests fulfilling the services assigned, covered by their garments, the whole picture is static and unfinished. Lifeless. "Since we live by the Spirit, let us keep in step with the Spirit" (Galatians 5:25).

—∿—

As you think about the colors God uses in His design for the priestly garments, what does each say to you about wearing His colors?

Blue

Scarlet

Purple

White

ARRAYED IN RIGHTEOUSNESS

"I delight greatly in the Lord;
my soul rejoices in my God.
For he has clothed me with garments of salvation
and arrayed me in a robe of his righteousness,
as a bridegroom adorns his head like a priest,
and as a bride adorns herself with her jewels" (Isaiah 61:10).

Further exploration of the design of the priests' garments show other elements of their construction, each rich and beautiful to the eye, and to the eye of the heart.

Gold

We find one metal in the priests' garments: gold. This was not fabric-dyed gold; rather, it was pure gold stretched into thin strands and woven, as embroidery, into the design.

Gold is indestructible and imperishable. It is stable and durable. Gold cannot be destroyed by fire. Gold can even stand immersion in salt water. It does not tarnish in air and it can resist almost any acid. The articles of gold discovered from ancient civilizations are of the same quality as when they were first made.

The gold we find in the priests' garments stands for eternal life. The writer of Hebrews says that Jesus has become High Priest "on the basis of the power of an indestructible life" (Hebrews 7:16).

Every believer has eternal life — eternal in quality (indestructible), not just quantity. Eternal life, eternally secured.

"I give them eternal life, and they shall never perish; no one will snatch them out of my hand. My Father, who has given them to me, is greater than all; no one can snatch them out of my Father's hand" (John 10:28).

Eternity is woven into the fabric of our lives. "He has also set eternity in the human heart" (Ecclesiastes 3:11). When we are clothed with power from on high, we are clothed in the power of eternity.

Linen

The priests' garments were made of linen, a fabric made from the fibers of the flax plant, in a time-consuming process,

"When they enter the gates of the inner court, they are to wear linen clothes; they must not wear any woolen garment while ministering at the gates of the inner court or inside the temple. They are to wear linen turbans on their heads and linen undergarments around their waists" (Ezekiel 44:17–18).

Linen stands for human nature, and *white* linen for human nature redeemed and purified.

"Fine linen, bright and clean, was given her to wear" (Revelation 19:8). Fine linen stands for the righteous acts of God's holy people.

The Holy Spirit has clothed *human beings* with power from on high. Not angelic beings. Not supernatural beings. Frail, weak humanity has been covered with the very power of heaven. Jesus was willing to dress Himself in human nature and to live and act in the power of the Holy Spirit so that He could become our great High Priest.

"For surely it is not angels he helps, but Abraham's descendants. For this reason he had to be made like them, fully human in every way, in order that he might become a merciful and faithful high priest in service to God, and that he might make atonement for the sins of the people" (Hebrews 2:16–17).

—⟋⟍—

Think about gold and linen as symbolic dressing, representing the Holy Spirit in your life. What does it mean to you today, in the midst of today's circumstances and challenges, that you are clothed in gold and fine linen?

DAY 3

"Tell all the skilled workers to whom I have given wisdom in such matters that they are to make garments for Aaron, for his consecration, so he may serve me as priest" (Exodus 28:3).

The rabbis established that the command for the priestly garments to be "for honor and for beauty" teach us that these garments were to be new and dignified. If the garments were defiled in any way, the priests could not conduct the service while wearing them. If they were to do so, the service would be invalid.

The rabbis determined that another aspect of "honor and beauty" meant that the uniform must fit each one exactly. The pants, for example, were not to be too long or too short. They were to cover the priest from hip to thigh. The whole thigh was to be covered (Exodus 28:42). The garments were tailor-made for each priest, created to fit his measurements. With the instructions for fitting being so exact, you can see why this would be necessary. If you and I wore the same dress size, it would still fit us each differently.

This hints at the tremendous workforce needed to turn out these garments in such quantities that every priest in Israel could be supplied with his own garments. There were so many priests available for duty that no priest ever offered the daily incense service more than once in his lifetime, and it was offered twice daily for many hundreds of years! Yet each had his own tailor-made garments. Each garment was as significant as the next.

These garments were made by skilled workers — trained, experienced, gifted workers — whose skill had been enhanced by supernaturally supplied wisdom. As was the way of the Holy Spirit under the Old Covenant, He came upon those appointed for this task while they performed it. It delights me to think of the Holy Spirit guiding every detail of the production of the clothing that was a picture of Him. He was creating a self-portrait.

OFF-THE-RACK OR TAILOR-MADE?

When the Holy Spirit clothes us with power from on high, though it is the same Spirit, He fits each of us differently. He adorns and empowers us in accordance with our gifts and calling. He directs us in our given circumstances. He speaks in ways specific to our unique personalities.

He is a living person. He is not inert. The symbols used to define Him — fire, water, wind — all suggest powerful movement, dynamic fluidity, instant agility. Anything but one-size-fits-all.

"Just as each of us has one body with many members, and these members do not all have the same function, so in Christ we, though many, form one body, and each member belongs to all the others. We have different gifts, according to the grace given to each of us" (Romans 12:4–6).

"Just as a body, though one, has many parts, but all its many parts form one body, so it is with Christ. For we were all baptized by one Spirit so as to form one body — whether Jews or Gentiles, slave or free — and we were all given the one Spirit to drink. Even so the body is not made up of one part but of many" (1 Corinthians 12:12–14).

We have the same Spirit, but His indwelling presence activates different gifts and different passions and different approaches. He does not make us clones of each other, but instead brings out our uniqueness.

He fits us together into a congruous entity made up of differing parts. The converging of the differing pieces gives the whole its beauty.

The gifts of His Spirit make us unique from each other, but the fruit of His Spirit is consistent.

"But the fruit of the Spirit is love, joy, peace, forbearance, kindness, goodness, faithfulness, gentleness and self-control.... Since we live by the Spirit, let us keep in step with the Spirit" (Galatians 5:22–23, 26).

Those who live by the Spirit will exhibit different gifts and expressions of those gifts, but the same fruit.

—m—

Do you see ways that the same Spirit expresses Himself in different ways through you than He does through others around you?

Is this good or bad? Why or why not?

Do you see the Spirit working out the same fruit in you as He is working out in others around you?

What consistencies to you see?

DAY 4

The Holy Spirit does work separately from Jesus and when He works, He makes Jesus the focus. One of His primary roles in our lives is to make Jesus real and present to us.

"When the Advocate comes, whom I will send to you from the Father — the Spirit of truth who goes out from the Father — he will testify about me" (John 15:26).

"He will not speak on his own; he will speak only what he hears, and he will tell you what is yet to come. He will glorify me because it is from me that he will receive what he will make known to you. All that belongs to the Father is mine. That is why I said the Spirit will receive from me what he will make known to you" (John 16:13–15).

Just as the priests did not wear their priestly garments outside the Tabernacle, or in any activity that was other than their priestly role, so the Holy Spirit does not anoint our lives or empower us apart from our relationship to Jesus. If we are not "in Christ," then the Holy Spirit is not in us.

THE JESUS WHISPERER

The Spirit's role is to make Jesus known; to be the one who interprets Jesus to our understanding. Remember how I compared the Holy Spirit to the voice that carries the Word?

I picture it something like this: Imagine an IV bag and the tube carrying the life-giving medications into the vein of a patient. The IV bag contains saline solution, and it is being fed into the vein because it is the substance that will deliver the medicine. When the medicine is injected into the tube, the saline carries that medicine into the body and causes it to flow in the bloodstream, giving the patient access to the medication his or her body needs. What gets the credit when the patient heals? The medicine the saline delivered.

The Holy Spirit is the vehicle through which Jesus is delivered to every part of your life. The Spirit takes all His cues from Jesus. Jesus said that the Spirit does not speak on His own, but speaks only what He hears; that the Spirit will glorify Jesus.

—⟩⟩⟩—

From the following Scripture passages, whom did Jesus claim as the source of His words?

John 14:24: *"These words you hear are not my own; they belong to the Father who sent me."*

John 14:10: *"The words I say to you I do not speak on my own authority. Rather, it is the Father, living in me, who is doing his work."*

John 17:8: *"For I gave them the words you gave me."*

John 12:49–50: *"For I did not speak on my own, but the Father who sent me commanded me to say all that I have spoken. I know that his command leads to eternal life. So whatever I say is just what the Father has told me to say."*

How does Jesus describe the Holy Spirit's role in our lives as modeled by the Father's role in Jesus' life?

"He will not speak on his own; he will speak only what he hears" (John 16:13).

Consider these statements in light of John 16:14–15 below.

"He will glorify me because it is from me that he will receive what he will make known to you. All that belongs to the Father is mine. That is why I said the Spirit will receive from me what he will make known to you."

The Spirit receives from _____ what He makes known to us.

Jesus receives from _____ what He makes know to us. ("Everything that I learned from my Father I have made known to you" [John 15:15]).

The Spirit will glorify _____ .

Jesus glorifies _____ .

("I have brought you glory on earth by finishing the work you gave me to do" [John 17:4].)

All that belongs to the Father belongs to _____ .

When the Spirit receives from Jesus and makes it known to us, from whom did Jesus receive it?

Do you agree that the Triune God — the Godhead — works in cooperation and unity? From the Father, through the Son, by the Spirit.

"For in Christ all the fullness [full to overflowing] of the Deity [Father and Spirit] lives in bodily form, and in Christ you have been brought to fullness [full to overflowing]" (Colossians 2:9–10). Let me restate it this way: Christ is full of the Father and the Spirit, and you are full of Christ.

THE TWO-LAYERED ANOINTING

"He then presented the other ram, the ram for the ordination, and Aaron and his sons laid their hands on its head. Moses slaughtered the ram and took some of its blood and put it on the lobe of Aaron's right ear, on the thumb of his right hand and on the big toe of his right foot. Moses also brought Aaron's sons forward and put some of the blood on the lobes of their right ears, on the thumbs of their right hands and on the big toes of their right feet" (Leviticus 8:22–24).

"Then Moses took some of the anointing oil and some of the blood from the altar and sprinkled them on Aaron and his garments and on his sons and their garments. So he consecrated Aaron and his garments and his sons and their garments" (Leviticus 8:30).

First the blood, then the oil. Scripture is consistent in the symbolism of the blood and oil: the blood represents Jesus who shed His blood for us, and the oil represents the Spirit. In the portion of the consecration ceremony called Ram of Ordination, Moses first anointed Aaron and his sons with blood. Specifically on the right ear, on the thumb of the right hand, and on the big toe of the right foot.

The anointing sanctified the ear, through which knowledge enters; then the thumb, the most important of the hand's five fingers and the one on which every other finger is dependent; then the toe, the balancing toe. This ceremony first covered all the ways a person interacts in obedience—hearing, doing, going. Then Moses sprinkled Aaron and his sons and their garments with both the anointing oil and the blood.

The blood reminds us of what Christ does for us—He forgives us of our sins; the oil reminds us of who Christ is in us—He cleanses us of the unrighteousness that causes us to sin. He redeems us from the power of sin, and cleanses us from the pollution of sin. One anointing is incomplete without the other.

The Holy Spirit does not come separate from Jesus, nor act apart from Jesus. He is to bring the living present Jesus into our experience and cause us to know and experience Him in our real-time living.

DAY 5

The Spirit is given to us to enable us to accomplish what the Father has called us to accomplish, and to be what Jesus has provided for us to be. He is not at our command, but He is available to us every single moment that we live. He is not passive and polite, but instead He is intrusive and demanding. Can we ignore Him? Yes. Can we grieve Him? Yes? Quench Him? Yes. Still He persistently gives chase. He clamors and wrestles and pursues because His love is stubborn and He is determined to deliver all of Jesus to us. When we accept what He is offering, we find ourselves living the life God has designed for us. Not a generic, off-the-rack life that might fit just anyone, but a tailor-made life that fits us perfectly.

LOVING LIFE

When the Spirit is unleashed in our lives through our complete surrender, He delivers more than we can ask or imagine. When we let the Spirit who is in us spill over into every area of our lives, we find that everything we have been working to find is waiting there in Him. We are invited to "be filled with the Spirit" (Ephesians 5:18). The verb tense makes it say, "Be constantly being filled with the Spirit." We are the recipients of the action; Jesus is the doer of the action. We are being filled; He is filling. When our lives are wide open to Him—like little birds with open beaks waiting expectantly for provision—He will fill us. Hear His invitation, "Open wide your mouth and I will fill it" (Psalm 81:10).

—m—

From the following statements, what does the Holy Spirit bring into our lives? As you identify each promise, consider what (1) What area of your life have you seen this promise clothe you? (2) What area of your life seems to be uncovered and needs to be clothed?

2 Corinthians 3:17: "Now the Lord is the Spirit, and where the Spirit of the Lord is, there is freedom."

Ephesians 3:16: "I pray that out of his glorious riches he may strengthen you with power through his Spirit in your inner being."

Romans 8:6: "The mind governed by the Spirit is life and peace."

WEEK THREE

 AS ONE

"'Gather the entire assembly at the entrance to the tent of meeting.' Moses did as the LORD commanded him, and the assembly gathered at the entrance to the tent of meeting" (Leviticus 8:3–4).

"When the day of Pentecost came, they were all together in one place" (Acts 2:1).

DAY I

God set out a meticulous ceremony of consecration to outfit the priests in their new garb. He didn't simply say, "Here. Put this on." He called all the people together to witness the solemn, holy occasion that opened a new chapter in the story of His work among His people. Though only five men would physically be fitted with the priestly garments at the consecration ceremony, they were representative of a line of priests. They were the firstfruits. The line of priests, and every priest in the priestly line, represented the nation of Israel. Every man, woman, and child in the nation was brought before God in the person of the priest.

COHERENCE

God wanted the whole nation to participate in the assembly and to know themselves to be part of a whole. He wanted His people unified and for their identity to be as a nation and a people. His design for His people was — and is — that they, though each is separate and unique, fuse into one body.

This consecration ceremony, then, was a consecration of all. I'm going to use the word *cohere* for this process because it means when things of a same kind attach to each other and form a solid whole.

One of the great miracles of the coming of the Spirit at Pentecost was the miracle of unity. The kind of unity to which we are called goes far beyond any kind of cooperation or agreement that human beings might reach with each other. God calls us to a unity that we are not able to produce. He wants coherence.

Read the following Scripture passages and then consider the questions below.

"So Christ himself gave the apostles, the prophets, the evangelists, the pastors and teachers, to equip his people for works of service, so that the body of Christ may be built up until we all reach unity in the faith and in the knowledge of the Son of God and become mature, attaining to the whole measure of the fullness of Christ" (Ephesians 4:11–13).

Who apportions and distributes the gifts of the Spirit to fill the roles of equippers?

What is the purpose of these gifts?

What is the mark of maturity in the faith and in the knowledge of Jesus?

What is essential to attaining the whole measure of the fullness of Christ?

"And God placed all things under his feet and appointed him to be head over everything for the church, which is his body, the fullness of him who fills everything in every way" (Ephesians 1:22–23).

Where is "the fullness of him who fills everything in every way" found?

DAY 2

God's plan is that His people will be as one, just as the Father, the Son, and the Spirit are as one. The Hebrew word Paul would have in mind as he wrote these passages from Ephesians that we looked at yesterday, is the word *echad*. It can have the sense of a "compound unity," or oneness derived from several elements. It is closely identified with yāhad — "to be united," according to the *Theological Wordbook of the Old Testament*. To help you see this more clearly, here are some ways the word *echad* is used when it means compound oneness.

*The people answered with **one voice** [kol echad] (Exodus 24:3).*

Then I will give to the peoples purified lips,
That all of them may call on the name of YHVH,
*To serve him with **one shoulder** [shechem echad] (Zephaniah 3:9).*

*The Hand of God was also on Judah to give them **one heart** [lev echad] (2 Chronicles 30:12).*

*[Adam and Eve] shall become **one flesh** [naphesh echad] (Genesis 2:24).*
*I will make them **an undivided nation** [goy echad] in the Land . . .*
***One single King** [melech echad] will be king for all of them,*
And they will no longer be two nations,
And they will no longer be divided into two kingdoms (Ezekiel 37:22).

When Jesus prayed for unity among His followers, He undoubtedly used the word *echad.* "that they may be one as we are one" (John 17:11).

—ɯ—

From this passage out of Jesus' prayer, answer the questions posed.

"I pray also for those who will believe in me through their message, that all of them may be one, Father, just as you are in me and I am in you. May they also be in us so that the world may believe that you have sent me. I have given them the glory that you gave me, that they may be one as we are one—I in them and you in me—so that they may be brought to complete unity. Then the world will know that you sent me and have loved them even as you have loved me" (John 17:20–23).

For whom is Jesus praying? How far out in time does this prayer extend?

Highlight or underline the phrases that Jesus uses to describe the *echad* of the Father and the Son.

Then underline or highlight the phrases that describe the *echad* Jesus will have with His disciples.

Then underline or highlight the phrase that speaks to the *echad* that He desires that His followers have with each other.

ON THAT DAY

Jesus so passionately desires unity among His followers that it is a main thrust of one of His final prayers on earth. This was on His mind as He faced His crucifixion. The whole full-spectrum plan of salvation for which He was about to die would not be finalized until it resulted in the miracle of a unified church. *Echad* was His heart's cry to the Father.

As Jesus explained the Holy Spirit to His disciples, pointing them to an upcoming day when the Spirit would descend to take up residence in them, He said this: "On that day you will realize that I am in my Father, and you are in me, and I am in you" (John 14:20). What did He mean by "on that day"? He was referring to the day when the Spirit came. That is when it would penetrate to their understanding and they would experience the *echad* that Jesus and the Father have. It is a unity so complete that He could state it as "you are in me," or He could say, "I am in you." If Jesus, by His Spirit, is in me, and the same Jesus is in you, then, in Him, you and I are *echad*—one.

Unity is such a powerful force that it could only be entrusted to a Spirit-filled church. In the wrong hands, the power of unity would be disastrous. Unity, even the kind that is nothing but flesh, is potent.

Let's look at the event that precipitated God's destruction of unity, which He then kept in storage until He could give it to His church.

Read Genesis 11:1−9 here, then answer the questions that follow.

Now the whole world had one language and a common speech. As people moved eastward, they found a plain in Shinar and settled there.

They said to each other, "Come, let's make bricks and bake them thoroughly." They used brick instead of stone, and tar for mortar. Then they said, "Come, let us build ourselves a city, with a tower that reaches to the heavens, so that we may make a name for ourselves; otherwise we will be scattered over the face of the whole earth."

But the LORD came down to see the city and the tower the people were building. The LORD said, "If as one people speaking the same language they have begun to do this, then nothing they plan to do will be impossible for them. Come, let us go down and confuse their language so they will not understand each other."

So the LORD scattered them from there over all the earth, and they stopped building the city. That is why it was called Babel — because there the LORD confused the language of the whole world. From there the LORD scattered them over the face of the whole earth.

What united "the whole world"?

What was the driving force behind their effort? "So that we may

_____   _____ ."

What was the Lord's evaluation of the situation? "If as one people speaking the same language they have begun to do this, then

_____

_____

_____ ."

What do you see as the power of unity, even apart from the Spirit's empowering?

Since their common language united them, what did the Lord do to create division?

Read Acts 2:4–12 here, then answer the questions that follow.

All of them were filled with the Holy Spirit and began to speak in other tongues as the Spirit enabled them.

Now there were staying in Jerusalem God-fearing Jews from every nation under heaven. When they heard this sound, a crowd came together in bewilderment, because each one heard their own language being spoken. Utterly amazed, they asked: "Aren't all these who are speaking Galileans? Then how is it that each of us hears them in our native language? Parthians, Medes and Elamites; residents of Mesopotamia, Judea and Cappadocia, Pontus and Asia, Phrygia and Pamphylia, Egypt and the parts of Libya near Cyrene; visitors from Rome (both Jews and converts to Judaism); Cretans and Arabs — we hear them declaring the wonders of God in our own tongues!" Amazed and perplexed, they asked one another, "What does this mean?"

The Scripture reports that Jews from _____ were staying in Jerusalem. How is this the reverse the incident at Babel?

At Babel, when one spoke, the other could not understand him. How is this reversed at Pentecost?

At Pentecost, when the Spirit gave utterance through the mouths of the Jesus followers, those words were understood in each person's own language. How is this a reversal of what occurred at Babel?

At Babel, the united people were seeking to create a name for themselves. What were the newly Spirit-filled people declaring at Pentecost?

When God released His Spirit onto the earth, one of the manifestations was that a diverse group of people were merged into a powerful force now called the church. The power of unity is such that God held it in reserve for His Spirit-enabled body. With that in mind, what do you think our enemy in the spiritual realm would target in his efforts to undermine God's agenda?

DAY 3

"Be completely humble and gentle; be patient, bearing with one another in love. Make every effort to keep the unity of the Spirit through the bond of peace. There is one body and one Spirit, just as you were called to one hope when you were called; one Lord, one faith, one baptism; one God and Father of all, who is over all and through all and in all" (Ephesians 4:2–6).

The Holy Spirit offers and calls us to a unity beyond our natural ability to produce. We are admonished to "make every effort to keep the unity of the Spirit." This unity is a gift of grace, but we are instructed to earnestly, diligently make *every* effort to guard and protect the unity that flows from the Spirit.

GUARD UNITY

When the priests were clothed in their garments, they were as one. Except for the High Priest, each priest's garments were identical to those of his brother priests. Their covering garments served to unite them. They were a compound unity—two elements fused into one—*echad*.

Unity has always been an anticipated outcome of our full salvation. It does not come naturally to us. The kinds of quarrels and offenses and hurt feelings that are the natural outflow of our human nature are the things that can disrupt unity and dilute the power of the church unified. That's why Paul warns us specifically to watch out for those things.

He instructs us to be humble and gentle, bearing with one another in love. A repeat of Galatians 5:22: "But the fruit of the Spirit is love, joy, peace, forbearance, kindness, goodness, faithfulness, gentleness and self-control." Not only does God command these attitudes, but He also supplies them. He has given us everything we need for life and godliness.

Give honest and prayerful thought to your interactions with others. What kinds of things disrupt unity for you? See how the Spirit might speak these words from Ephesians to you.

Has someone hurt your feelings? What is the Lord saying about that right now?

Do you find someone's personality abrasive? What is the Lord saying to you about that right now?

Do you feel dismissed by someone? What is the Lord saying to you about that right now?

Have you cut someone out of your life? What is the Lord saying to you about that right now?

Have you gossiped or delighted in passing along information about someone? What is the Lord saying to you about that right now?

What else is the Spirit convicting you about right now in terms of guarding the unity He so highly prizes?

—⚬—

Paul's instruction is to keep the unity, or to guard it. When you are guarding something valuable, do you wait until a threat is upon it and then respond? Or do you stand lookout and watch for danger, assailing it before it reaches your gates? "The prudent see danger and take refuge, but the simple keep going and pay the penalty" (Proverbs 22:3).

At the first stirrings of resentment or hurt or anger, we can take evasive action. Recognize the emotion. Admit it. Let the Spirit direct you in love and forbearance instead of letting your emotions drag you down a road of resentment and anger. The response might be justified if your goal is to protect your feelings, but if your goal is to protect the unity of the Spirit, then do the spiritual work that will keep unity in place.

Paul makes clear that guarding the unity will require attitudes that flow from the Spirit, like humility and patience and understanding. He says that the unity will be guarded within the bonds of peace.

Have you ever noticed that your own inner peace makes you able to live at peace with others? When your peace is gone, you are likely to infect those closest to you with that inner chaos. Why is it that when I am in a "bad mood," I feel free to take it out on others? We preserve unity within the bonds of peace. If you have identified a place where you are not guarding the unity, might it hint to you that there is a place in you that is lacking peace? What would it mean for the Spirit to provide peace in that place of your heart?

"Let us therefore make every effort to do what leads to peace and to mutual edification" (Romans 14:19).

DAY 4

"Now if you obey me fully and keep my covenant, then out of all nations you will be my treasured possession. Although the whole earth is mine, you will be for me a kingdom of priests and a holy nation" (Exodus 19:5–6).

On that first Pentecost, at the giving of the Torah, God called a band of escaped slaves — the Israelites — and forged them into a nation. When God proposed to His people, and took them as His own, that covenant relationship set them apart from all the other nations on earth and made them a unified, set apart nation. "You are to be holy to me because I, the Lord, am holy, and I have set you apart from the nations to be my own" (Leviticus 20:26).

Torah — given at the covenant ceremony — bound the people together and served as their wisdom among the nations. It put them at odds with other nations, and singled them out as a nation apart. Their set-apart-ness was the ground of their unity.

On the great day of Pentecost when the Holy Spirit fell on the gathered believers, the Torah of Mount Sinai moved into the hearts and lives of God's people and redefined them and radicalized them. They were so transformed that it set them apart from others who did not have the Spirit of God in them. They became a unified force advancing the kingdom of God and pushing back gates of hell.

BUILDING BLOCKS OF UNITY

The Scripture uses the analogy of a building. Each of us is cemented to the other by the Holy Spirit. We are interdependent and the fullness of our strength and stability comes from our connectedness. This is by His design. It is not an indication of weakness to lean on one another, but of strength. It is in this building—this conjoined structure—that God lives fully by His Spirit, and that we act as His priests.

"In him [Jesus] the whole building is joined together and rises to become a holy temple in the Lord. And in him you too are being built together to become a dwelling in which God lives by his Spirit" (Ephesians 2:21–22).

"As you come to him, the living Stone — rejected by humans but chosen by God and precious to him — you also, like living stones, are being built into a spiritual house to be a holy priesthood, offering spiritual sacrifices acceptable to God through Jesus Christ" (1 Peter 2:4–5).

Each of us matters. Each of us is responsible for addressing our own situations that break unity because others are depending on us. See how specifically God illustrates the oneness of the many. The *echad* He desires.

—⚭—

Consider how you are stronger because of the other "living stones" around you. Think back as far as you can and write down names of "living stones" from your life. You might consider contacting them to let them know that they have been a "living stone" to you.

For whom are you a "living stone"? Who has God put in the orbit of your life and has allowed or is allowing you to be a rock to them?

—ɯ—

See that the Scripture uses the metaphor of living stones and priests at the same time. The same Holy Spirit who clothes you with power also cements you into the building in which God lives by His Spirit. If we long for the fullness of the Spirit, and all the power He brings from on high, then we must be intimately connected to the body of Christ — the church.

DAY 5

"Once the priests enter the holy precincts, they are not to go into the outer court until they leave behind the garments in which they minister, for these are holy. They are to put on other clothes before they go near the places that are for the people" (Ezekiel 42:14).

"When they go out into the outer court where the people are, they are to take off the clothes they have been ministering in and are to leave them in the sacred rooms, and put on other clothes, so that the people are not consecrated through contact with their garments" (Ezekiel 44:19).

In the Old Testament, where the picture of the reality we know now is painted, the priests were not to wear their garments outside the Tabernacle or the Temple. Notice the curious explanation of why they are not to walk among the people in their consecrated garments:

"so that the people are not consecrated through contact with their garments."

The holy garments were so powerful and effectual that if the people came into contact with them, they would become consecrated just by touching them. That's how powerful the shadow was. Imagine the Substance! The Holy Spirit covering our lives is the reality of which the priest's garments spoke.

We don't have the same restrictions as did the priests of the Old Covenant. We are in the era where we are a kingdom of priests, sent out clothed with power that resides in us and on us. As we live and move among one another, the Holy Spirit rests on us in such power that we influence one another just by being present to each other. We don't have to have the right words to say or the answer to a problem or the solution to a dilemma. We are in such supernatural unity through the Holy Spirit that often just being together releases a dimension of power that is different than what we experience in solitude. Certainly we are called to seek God in solitude and individually, but the call to seek Him together is equally compelling.

THE HEM OF HIS GARMENT

And wherever he went — into villages, towns or countryside — they placed the sick in the marketplaces. They begged him to let them touch even the edge of his cloak, and all who touched it were healed (Mark 6:56).

Do you remember the story of the woman with an issue of blood who touched the edge of His garment and was immediately healed? This would have been the *tzitzit* (ritually knotted fringes) on the hem of His outer garment. It was a common understanding that to grab hold of a rabbi's *tzitzit* would access that rabbi's anointing. As Mark tells this story, he adds some interesting details.

"Immediately her bleeding stopped and she felt in her body that she was freed from her suffering. At once Jesus realized that power had gone out from him. He turned around in the crowd and asked, 'Who touched my clothes?'" (5:29–30).

Mark indicates that at the moment she came into contact with His garment, she was healed. At that same moment, Jesus realized power had gone out from Him. Consider this with me. Power flowed from Him into her. Two questions: (1) Were Jesus' clothes magical? In other words, did His clothes cure her? (2) When Jesus felt power leave Him, does that mean that He had a fixed limit of power and now He was low? Did His power have to be replenished, or did He live being filled at all times with the Spirit?

I suggest that Jesus' robe with its Torah — prescribed *tzitzit* on each corner — was a picture of the Holy Spirit who covered and filled Him. We have already looked at the scriptural evidence that Jesus did all His work on earth through the power of the Spirit, so this healing would also have been in the power of the Spirit. It shows that when she came into contact with Him through faith, she had come into contact with the Holy Spirit in Him. The very life in Him flowed into her. Not something apart from Him, but the very Spirit who indwelled and empowered Him flowed from Him to her and produced healing. It was such a dynamic interaction that not only did she feel the inflow, but Jesus felt the outflow.

"God anointed Jesus of Nazareth with the Holy Spirit and power, and how he went around doing good and healing all who were under the power of the devil, because God was with him" (Acts 10:38).

Let me push the idea further. If Jesus dwells in you and lives His life through you, then the Spirit that clothes you with power, clothes you with *His* power. Power from on high. God can bring people into contact with Jesus through you. You are dressed in Him and clothed with His power.

I am not suggesting that you are Jesus — or that by touching your clothes others might be healed of their illnesses. I'm just saying, could this be on the eternal record to remind us and assure us that the more we learn to live in the Spirit's flow, as we interact with each other, there is a way that His Spirit operates *among us* that is unique.

"Again, truly I tell you that if two of you on earth agree about anything they ask for, it will be done for them by my Father in heaven. For where two or three gather in my name, there am I with them" (Matthew 18:19–20).

"His intent was that now, **through the church,** *the manifold wisdom of God should be made known to the rulers and authorities in the heavenly realms, according to his eternal purpose that he accomplished in Christ Jesus our Lord"* (Ephesians 3:10–11).

Time after time, the Holy Spirit acted in specific and unusual ways when the church was gathered. The power of unity cannot be overstated.

"While they were worshiping the Lord and fasting, the Holy Spirit said, 'Set apart for me Barnabas and Saul for the work to which I have called them'" (Acts 13:2).

"After they prayed, the place where they were meeting was shaken. And they were all filled with the Holy Spirit and spoke the word of God boldly" (Acts 4:31).

One function of the priests' garments was to make them one. The presence of the Holy Spirit covering us makes us one.

"There is one body and **one Spirit,** *just as you were called to one hope when you were called; one Lord, one faith, one baptism; one God and Father of all, who is over all and through all and in all"* (Ephesians 4:4–6; author's emphasis).

How does the Holy Spirit clothing you with power create supernatural unity?

How have you seen the power of unity in your walk in the Spirit?

WEEK FOUR

 CLEAN, RIGHTEOUS, STRONG

"To him who is able to keep you from stumbling and to present you before his glorious presence without fault and with great joy — to the only God our Savior be glory, majesty, power and authority, through Jesus Christ our Lord, before all ages, now and forevermore! Amen" (Jude 24–25).

DAY 1

This week we'll consider the priest's garments in the order which they were put on them during the consecration ceremony.

Moses said to the assembly, "This is what the LORD has commanded to be done." Then Moses brought Aaron and his sons forward and washed them with water. He put the tunic on Aaron, tied the sash around him. (Leviticus 8:5–7).

"Weave the tunic of fine linen. . . . The sash is to be the work of an embroiderer. . . . Make linen undergarments as a covering for the body, reaching from the waist to the thigh. Aaron and his sons must wear them whenever they enter the tent of meeting or approach the altar to minister in the Holy Place, so that they will not incur guilt and die" (Exodus 28:39; 42–43).

The first action of the consecration ceremony was a *mikveh.* Their whole bodies were to be washed with water. From then on, they only had to wash hands and feet at the Laver of Cleansing in the Tabernacle courtyard. But, before being clothed with power, there was a head-to-toe cleansing. The symbolism of the water cleansing the body was pointing to the reality of being immersed fully in the Holy Spirit, who would cleanse the inward man.

Jesus entered into His priestly *mikveh* in the Jordan River at the age of 30. Thirty years old was the age at which a man could assume his full duties as priest. At Jesus' public baptism, the Holy Spirit descended on Him in the bodily form of a dove. The Holy Spirit had always been in Him. He was born of the Holy Spirit and was led by the Spirit all His life. But at His baptism the Spirit it seems the Spirit came upon Him in a new way. He performed no miracles or ministry before His baptism, but afterward began to teach and heal with such power that those who had known Him all His life, as Mary and Joseph's son, wondered where all this wisdom came from.

Jesus had no need of cleansing, but His public *mikveh* was in accordance with the statutes of God. "This is what the Lord has commanded to be done," Moses had said. I think that Jesus said something like that to John the Baptist (Matthew 3:15).

When we are baptized by the Holy Spirit, we are submerged into Him so that He not only fills us, but He also covers us. This is the beginning—to be cleansed in every part of our personality, our conscience, our heart and mind.

—⟋⟍—

Taking into account that the priests were fully cleansed at their consecration, and afterward washed hands and feet in the Laver of Cleansing in the Tabernacle courtyard, what do you think Jesus meant to convey to His disciples on the night of the final Passover?

"He came to Simon Peter, who said to him, 'Lord, are you going to wash my feet?'"

Jesus replied, "You do not realize now what I am doing, but later you will understand."

"No," said Peter, "you shall never wash my feet."

Jesus answered, "Unless I wash you, you have no part with me."

"Then, Lord," Simon Peter replied, "not just my feet but my hands and my head as well!"

Jesus answered, "Those who have had a bath need only to wash their feet; their whole body is clean. And you are clean."

"You are already clean because of the word I have spoken to you" (John 13:6–10; 15:3).

—‿‿—

Because you have accepted Jesus as your Lord, and He has baptized you in His Spirit, you are clean. You might not *feel* clean, but Jesus says you *are*. You are clean on the inside, but He will continue to wash your hands and feet—those parts of you that come into contact with the world. He will continually cleanse you of the grime that clings to you as you live life. But you are washed and clean.

DAY 2

A fter the *mikveh*, Moses put the tunic on Aaron first, the High Priest representing all priests. The first thing to note is that Moses put the tunic and the other garments on Aaron. He did not hand the garments to Aaron and instruct him to put them on. In the same way, it is the Father who clothes us with power from on high, and who, through the Son, pours out the Spirit.

We are told very little about the tunic. It is made of fine linen and is woven, not pieced together by sewing. The linen speaks of human nature, the white of the linen speaks of human nature purified. The foundation of the garments is purity and holiness. Symbolically, nothing is layered on until purity is in place.

The Hebrew word here translated "tunic" is from a root meaning "to cover" or "to hide." It is the same word used in Genesis 3:21 to say, "The Lord God made *garments* of skin for Adam and his wife and clothed them; author's emphasis." He covered their shame. Just like Moses covered Aaron with a covering of purity that he did not possess intrinsically, so the Lord God covered Adam and Eve with a covering they could not produce. And He covers us with the blood of Christ so that we are made clean and pure in His sight. All Him. His idea, His activity, His doing.

In the Book of Revelation, when the heavenly realm opened to John and he records what heaven sees, he sees those who "have washed their robes and made them white in the blood of the Lamb" (Revelation 7:14).

The white fine linen covering tells us that the Holy Spirit's first and foundational work is to purify us. In the *mikveh*, our sins have been washed away. We have a fresh start. Immediately the linen robe is added. This demonstrates that, on top of washing us clean from our sins, the Spirit will do a work of purifying the unrighteousness that *causes* sin. "If we confess our sins, he is faithful and just and will *forgive us our sins and purify us from all unrighteousness*" (1 John 1:9; author emphasis).

—ꟷ—

Answer these questions based on this statement.
"For he chose us in him before the creation of the world to be holy and blameless in his sight" (Ephesians 1:4).

For what purpose did He choose us?

What does it mean that He chose us "in Christ"?

Does our holiness come from ourselves?

If God chose us so that He could make us holy and blameless, do you think He knows what He's doing? Can He accomplish what He sets out to do?

Take a few minutes right now to focus on the covering tunic the Spirit has clothed you in. Accept His gift of Himself, through whom you can be holy and blameless. You are covered in pure white linen.

DAY 3

BELTED IN

The tunic was secured by a sash or belt that was made of linen and was embroidered in crimson, blue, and purple. "The sash was made of finely twisted linen and blue, purple and scarlet yarn — the work of an embroiderer — as the LORD commanded Moses" (Exodus 39:29).

The colors are the same as found throughout the Tabernacle. Crimson for the humanity of Jesus and the blood He shed for our redemption; blue for His divine nature; and purple, the combination of the two, standing for His eternal kingship. (See Week 2, Day 2.)

This belt held the tunic, or covering — or righteousness — in place. His very Person, made real and present by His Spirit, holds the covering in place.

"To him who is able to keep you from stumbling and to present you before his glorious presence without fault and with great joy — to the only God our Savior be glory, majesty, power and authority, through Jesus Christ our Lord, before all ages, now and forevermore! Amen" (Jude 24–25).

Speaking of the Messiah, Isaiah says, "The Spirit of the Lord will rest on him, . . . Righteousness will be his belt and faithfulness the sash around his waist" (Isaiah 11:2; 5). When we are clothed with power from on high, the sash that holds our holiness in place is Jesus, the Righteous and Faithful.

—◊◊◊—

Consider the sash that is holding your holiness and purity in place. Jesus Himself who has finished all the work of redemption, typified in the crimson, blue, and purple woven together into a work of art.

—◊◊◊—

The tunic and its belt were the garments both of the High Priest and also of the priests. The High Priest had more and more elaborate garments that were to fit over his white linen robe, but the ordinary priests had just the tunic and belt. When the Holy Spirit clothes us with power from on high, we are clothed with the fullness of Jesus — so, each of the garments will show us the Holy Spirit in your life, He brings all of Christ to bear on all of you. But there is a beautiful message being conveyed in this picture of the garments of the ordinary priests.

The High Priest has four more layers to his garments. His white linen tunic and its linen belt are known as the white garments and the remaining four layers are called the golden garments. For a few moments each day, the High Priest is arrayed just like the ordinary priests. The only other time that the High Priest is in his white garments alone is on the Day of Atonement when he enters the Holy of Holies to offer the blood of the atonement sacrifice.

Our Great High Priest was willing to become like us so that we could become like Him.

"Since the children have flesh and blood, he too shared in their humanity so that by his death he might break the power of him who holds the power of death — that is, the devil — and free those who all their lives were held in slavery by their fear of death. For surely it is not angels he helps, but Abraham's descendants. For this reason he had to be made like them, fully human in every way, in order that he might become a merciful and faithful high priest in service to God, and that he might make atonement for the sins of the people. Because he himself suffered when he was tempted, he is able to help those who are being tempted" (Hebrews 2:14–18).

"The Word became flesh and made his dwelling among us. We have seen his glory, the glory of the one and only Son, who came from the Father, full of grace and truth" (John 1:14).

THE WHITE GARMENTS ON
THE DAY OF ATONEMENT

"This is how Aaron is to enter the Most Holy Place: He must first bring a young bull for a sin offering and a ram for a burnt offering. He is to put on the sacred linen tunic, with linen undergarments next to his body; he is to tie the linen sash around him and put on the linen turban" (Leviticus 16:3–4).

The only time during the year that the High Priest performed duties in the white garments without the covering of the golden garments was when he offered the blood of the atonement sacrifice in the Holy of Holies, where the Shikenah Presence of God dwelt. This pictures the reality that when Jesus became both our High Priest making the offering, and the atonement sacrifice — when He offered Himself — He was dressed in weak, frail flesh. He laid aside His rightful regalia in heaven and entered earth dressed in mere clay. In His white garments — His humanity — without His kingly position or His heavenly power, He offered Himself as the sacrifice for our sin.

You wrapped Your gift in flesh and blood. The Wrapping was such that it invited us into the Gift. Had You sent Your Son unwrapped, we could not have seen Him because the brightness of His countenance would have blinded us. Like the Israelites of old, we would have hidden our faces from Him in fear and shame.

The angels know Him wrapped in eternal glory and royal robes. They saw Him before He took upon Himself the form of a servant and was made in the likeness of men. The angels saw His triumphant return to the glory He had before the world began, and see Him now in His exalted form.

But we see Him in the flawless beauty of His humanity. We see the grandeur of His Incarnation, when He demonstrated the enormity of His love for us by wrapping Himself in flesh and blood so that He could destroy that which held us captive. Seeing Him, we are blinded by His beauty to anything other than Him.

We will someday see Your indescribable Gift as the angels see Him. I know that sight will be a different beauty than I have ever known. But I cannot imagine that it will be more breathtakingly beautiful to me than the King of kings wrapped in flesh and blood for my sake. (*Pursuing the Christ*, Jennifer Kennedy Dean)

—◊◊◊—

What message do you see enacted when you see that underneath the golden garments — beautifully embroidered with gold woven throughout—is the same linen tunic and linen belt worn by the ordinary priests?

What does it say to you right now in your life?

TRANSFIGURED

"Jesus took Peter, James and John with him and led them up a high mountain, where they were all alone. There he was transfigured before them. His clothes became dazzling white, whiter than anyone in the world could bleach them. And there appeared before them Elijah and Moses, who were talking with Jesus. . . . Then a cloud appeared and covered them, and a voice came from the cloud: "This is my Son, whom I love. Listen to him!" (Mark 9:2–7).

In this incident, which occurred in the waning days of Jesus' ministry in the flesh, Jesus' countenance and the skin on His body shone so brightly that His robes even became dazzling white. For this moment, the glory of heaven hidden behind the veil of His flesh, flashed through. To complete the picture, a cloud—the same cloud of God's presence that had appeared on Mount Sinai—appeared and God once again spoke from the cloud. He spoke from Isaiah 42:1. "Here is my servant, whom I uphold, my chosen one in whom I delight; *I will put my Spirit on him."* God used these words that were familiar to the men chosen to be the witnesses of this holy event. They understood Him to be calling Jesus the promised Messiah. God affirmed that Jesus in His earthly ministry would be anointed with the Spirit.

When Jesus was transfigured, His true nature—what He was inside—broke through to change the appearance of His outside. His divine nature showed through the veil of His flesh. When we see Him, through the eyes of our hearts, in His incarnate state, remember that He veiled His glory and came to us so that we would be able to look upon His face.

DAY 4

"Make the robe of the ephod entirely of blue cloth, with an opening for the head in its center. There shall be a woven edge like a collar around this opening, so that it will not tear. Make pomegranates of blue, purple and scarlet yarn around the hem of the robe, with gold bells between them. The gold bells and the pomegranates are to alternate around the hem of the robe. Aaron must wear it when he ministers. The sound of the bells will be heard when he enters the Holy Place before the LORD *and when he comes out, so that he will not die"* (Exodus 28:31–35).

The robe covered the High Priest's linen tunic. It was made entirely of blue, representing Christ's heavenly origins and divine nature. In this picture we are reminded that after His incarnation, He was exalted to His former place of glory. His human nature and His divine nature were now fused into one unique nature, but the divine covers the human.

"And now, Father, glorify me in your presence with the glory I had with you before the world began" (John 17:5).

"After he said this, he was taken up before their very eyes, and a cloud hid him from their sight" (Acts 1:9).

"After he had provided purification for sins, he sat down at the right hand of the Majesty in heaven" (Hebrews 1:3).

"He raised Christ from the dead and seated him at his right hand in the heavenly realms, far above all rule and authority, power and dominion, and every name that is invoked, not only in the present age but also in the one to come. And God placed all things under his feet and appointed him to be head over everything for the church, which is his body, the fullness of him who fills everything in every way" (Ephesians 1:20–23).

When Jesus poured out the Holy Spirit, the promise of the Father, He poured out from His exalted divine life. He clothed us in His heavenly life. I don't mean that He made us gods, or that *we* are Jesus, but that we — in our weak flesh — *are* dressed in His divine nature and power.

But because of his great love for us, God, who is rich in mercy, made us alive with Christ even when we were dead in transgressions — it is by grace you have been saved. And God raised us up with Christ and seated us with him in the heavenly realms in Christ Jesus, in order that in the coming ages he might show the incomparable riches of his grace, expressed in his kindness to us in Christ Jesus" (Ephesians 2:4–7).

Through His Spirit, you already have access to the eternal resources of God, the spiritual aspects of reality. The Spirit delivers them into your life. God's promises are not for someday. They're for today. Faith is looking forward to a future, but also it is living fully supplied in the present. We are to walk in faith by keeping in step with the Spirit.

—〜〜—

From the following Scriptures, identify phrases that tell you that heaven's resources are available to you on earth, in the present moment.

"For he has rescued us from the dominion of darkness and brought us into the kingdom of the Son he loves" (Colossians 1:13).

"Praise be to the God and Father of our Lord Jesus Christ, who has blessed us in the heavenly realms with every spiritual blessing in Christ" (Ephesians 1:3).

"And God raised us up with Christ and seated us with him in the heavenly realms in Christ Jesus" (Ephesians 2:6).

"For you died, and your life is now hidden with Christ in God" (Colossians 3:3).

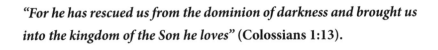

When God's Word speaks of the spiritual world, of the resources of the heavenly realm, the action is spoken of as already completed. The Spirit brings the available resources of God into our lives.

SEAMLESS

The robe was to be woven of one piece. No seams. This hints to us of His eternal nature. He has always been and will always be. His is an eternal, seamless life. He was from the beginning and will never die.

Hebrews 9:14 calls the Holy Spirit "the eternal spirit." He is the Spirit of Jesus, and He is God, and so He is eternal. "Eternal" means "has no beginning and has no end." Seamless.

Because you are clothed with power from on high and covered in the life of the Spirit, you are dealing with temporal circumstance *with eternal power and perspective.* The promise of eternal life goes far beyond where you go when you die, but embraces eternity now. "Fight the good fight of the faith. Take hold of the eternal life to which you were called when you made your good confession in the presence of many witnesses" (1 Timothy 6:12). Live eternal life every day as you keep in step with the eternal Spirit.

When we telescope time down to pinpoint our little moment and keep the focus there, then we miss out on the power, freedom, and peace of an eternal outlook. We can easily become obsessed with me, mine, I, and miss what God is doing. Because you are clothed with heaven's own power, you can look up, and look around, and settle your heart into an eternal rhythm.

—〰—

Consider some ways that your perspective might change if you looked at things in light of eternity. Ask the Eternal Spirit to bring light.

Values

Possessions

Relationships

Struggles

.

Other

HEADSTRONG

The robe had an opening for the head: "There shall be a woven edge like a collar around this opening, so that it will not tear." The robe was fitted for the head. Its opening was designed so that it would leave the head on display, with the garments as the dressing for that which the head directed.

Jesus is the Head. He is guiding and directing through His Spirit every step we take, every thought we think, every word we speak. If we are yielded to Him, He is there for us in ways we can't even imagine.

"And God placed all things under his feet and appointed him to be head over everything for the church, which is his body, the fullness of him who fills everything in every way" (Ephesians 1:22–23).

—⟋Ⱳ⟍—

Look carefully at the passage in Ephesians that tells us that Jesus is the Head. Based on this passage, answer the questions that follow.

"I keep asking that the God of our Lord Jesus Christ, the glorious Father, may give you the Spirit of wisdom and revelation, so that you may know him better. I pray that the eyes of your heart may be enlightened in order that you may know the hope to which he has called you, the riches of his glorious inheritance in his holy people, and his incomparably great power for us who believe. That power is the same as the mighty strength he exerted when he raised Christ from the dead and seated him at his right hand in the heavenly realms, far above all rule and authority, power and dominion, and every name that is invoked, not only in the present age but also in the one to come. And God placed all things under his feet and appointed him to be head over everything for the church, which is his body, the fullness of him who fills everything in every way" (Ephesians 1:17–23).

How is the Spirit described? "The Spirit of _____

_____ ."

What does that mean to you?

What does Paul identify as the purpose of the Spirit in you? "So that you may _____."

Once you heart's eyes are enlightened to understand the spiritual realm, what three things will you come to know? What does each of these show you about the Spirit in your life?

One thing the Spirit will reveal is His "incomparably great power for us who believe." Underline or highlight the description of that power.

One thing you will have underlined is: *"That power is the same as the mighty strength he exerted when he raised Christ from the dead."* How did God raise Jesus? (See Romans 8:11.)

How does this passage show you that the Holy Spirit makes the reality of Christ our experience?

—☙—

The head directs everything the body does, from making decisions deliberately, to causing the eyes to blink. The Holy Spirit is delivering the thoughts and directions of Jesus to our lives without intermission.

During my husband's struggle with brain cancer, I wrote this in my journal:

> *Wayne, because he is not able to exercise discipline over his brain right now, does not know he has a left side again. It is foreign to him. In the course of his hallucinating, he looks at his left hand and says, "What is that?" Once he called me from across the room and said, "Jennifer! You need to move your hand. It's in my way!" Several times I have seen him lift his left hand with his right hand and try to move it out of his way as if it were an object sitting on his lap. How strange that his hand is connected to his body in every way except that it is not receiving signals from his brain.*
>
> *As I watched Wayne today, grieved as I was, I could not help but think about the way the Scripture describes the relationship between Christ and His followers. He is the Head and we are the body. See how totally each part of the body is dependent upon the Head? He moves through His believers and His desires and will are exercised through His followers. Without the Head, the hand cannot be the hand; the foot cannot be the foot. The apostle Paul wrote about a follower who starts living as if he or she were in charge. "He has lost connection with the Head, from whom the whole body, supported and held together by its ligaments and sinews, grows as God causes it to grow" (Col 1:19). A body part disconnected from its Head is lifeless—as useless as if it belonged to someone else.*

As we see Christ as the Head, with His impulses and thoughts being delivered to us by His Spirit, we can get a glimpse of the power, peace, and freedom He has available to deliver if we just receive. The very power of heaven, the power that raised Jesus from the dead, the power that exalted Him over every other principality . . . all that power can be delivered to our lives through the Spirit. Eternal power.

ARMORED

"There shall be a woven edge like a collar around this opening, so that it will not tear." The word translated "collar" is sometimes used for "a coat of mail." NASB translates it like this: "There shall be an opening at its top in the middle of it; around its opening there shall be a binding of woven work, like the opening of a coat of mail, so that it will not be torn."

The language used to describe the collar, or opening, can also be a military term used to describe garments meant to protect and to deflect enemy weapons. The Holy Spirit, who covers us in heaven's own power and eternal, indestructible life, acts in our lives like a coat of mail.

Paul, using a metaphor of his day—though it is likely a concept internalized from his early learning about the priest's garments—to bring out the truths of the priest's garments, writes about the armor of God. In that discourse, he says: "In addition to all this, take up the shield of faith, with which you can extinguish all the flaming arrows of the evil one" (Ephesians 6:16).

The Holy Spirit has covered you with an impenetrable armor. He is a protection over your life. That doesn't mean that no difficulties, challenges, or sorrows will come your way, but that nothing that comes your way can defeat you. It means that nothing can come into your experience that He can't turn around and use to enrich, enhance, and bless you. Remember that your coat of mail is eternal. He will outlast any onslaught without weakening.

"Make pomegranates of blue, purple and scarlet yarn around the hem of the robe, with gold bells between them. The gold bells and the pomegranates are to alternate around the hem of the robe. Aaron must wear it when he ministers. The sound of the bells will be heard when he enters the Holy Place before the LORD and when he comes out, so that he will not die" (Exodus 28:33–35).

FRUITFUL

Around the hem of the robe were to be woven pomegranates and gold bells. They were to alternate around the bottom of the robe. Notice that the pomegranates were to be made of the familiar combination of blue, purple, and scarlet. They represent, then, something of the work of salvation fully accomplished by Jesus. The bells are made of gold. Gold signifies eternity, and purity, and strength.

Clearly, the bells and the pomegranates are to tell a story together. There were the same number of bells as there were pomegranates.

Before we get to what the decorative hem is illustrating, let me clarify something. Notice the statements that say: "Aaron must wear it when he ministers. The sound of the bells will be heard when he enters the Holy Place before the Lord and when he comes out, so that he will not die."

Like all the other priestly garments, Aaron is instructed to wear this robe with its decorative bells whenever he is in the holy place — not the Holy of Holies. He does not wear the robe into the Holy of Holies, which he enters once a year clad in the white garments. The people are reminded here that unless Aaron is covered in his priestly garments that consecrate him, he will die in the presence of the Lord.

It is not true that the bells were so the people would know that he had not died, but so that he would not die. From the wording, it sounds to me as if the sound was for the Lord to hear, not the people.

I think that the bells represent our faith, the testing of which is more precious than gold, and the pomegranates represent our Spirit-born works. Fruit is a metaphor referring to the natural manifestation of something. For example an apple is the natural manifestation of an apple tree. The natural manifestation of faith is deeds that reflect that faith.

Faith and works are not mutually exclusive, unless we are working for approval. When we have evidence (works) in our lives that flow out of the divine life of the Spirit acting through us, it brings honor to Jesus.

"Let your light shine before others, that they may see *your good deeds and* glorify *your Father in heaven"* (Matthew 5:16).

"For we are God's handiwork, created in Christ Jesus to do good works, which God prepared in advance for us to do" (Ephesians 2:10).

Again, we are not referring to works for salvation, or even works to keep salvation, but rather the kinds of deeds that naturally flow from the divine life of Jesus in you, empowered by His Spirit. You don't need to "work" or strain to work. You need to rest to work. The deeper you rest, the more powerfully you will work. Rest in Him and His powerful life in you and let Him empower and enable you to walk in Him.

—⟋⟍—

Go through James 2:14–26 thought by thought and notice what James has to say about faith and works as they operate in balance to each other.

"What good is it, my brothers and sisters, if someone claims to have faith but has no deeds? Can such faith save them? Suppose a brother or a sister is without clothes and daily food. If one of you says to them, 'Go in peace; keep warm and well fed,' but does nothing about their physical needs, what good is it? In the same way, faith by itself, if it is not accompanied by action, is dead.

But someone will say, 'You have faith; I have deeds.'

Show me your faith without deeds, and I will show you my faith by my deeds. You believe that there is one God. Good! Even the demons believe that — and shudder.

You foolish person, do you want evidence that faith without deeds is useless? Was not our father Abraham considered righteous for what he did when he offered his son Isaac on the altar? You see that his faith and his actions were working together, and his faith was made complete by what he did. And the scripture was fulfilled that says, 'Abraham believed God, and it was credited to him as righteousness,' and he was called God's friend. You see that a person is considered righteous by what they do and not by faith alone.

In the same way, was not even Rahab the prostitute considered righteous for what she did when she gave lodging to the spies and sent them off in a different direction? As the body without the spirit is dead, so faith without deeds is dead."

—⟋⟍—

Faith and deeds produced by faith are the balance of the life lived in the Spirit. Our faith expressed in actions that prove the presence of Jesus in our lives, adorn our lives and show our invisible faith in visible ways.

Think about the things you do or words you say that you know were generated by the Spirit in you. Are these not proofs to you that the Spirit is working mightily in you and through you? Faith and works are a compound whole. Neither complete without the other. *Echad.*

WEEK FIVE

 MADE ONE

"For God was pleased to have all his fullness dwell in him, and through him to reconcile to himself all things, whether things on earth or things in heaven, by making peace through his blood, shed on the cross (Colossians 1:19–20).

"With all wisdom and understanding, he made known to us the mystery of his will according to his good pleasure, which he purposed in Christ, to be put into effect when the times reach their fulfillment — to bring unity to all things in heaven and on earth under Christ" (Ephesians 1:8–10).

DAY I

EPHOD

"Make the ephod of gold, and of blue, purple and scarlet yarn, and of finely twisted linen — the work of skilled hands" (Exodus 28:6).

GOLDEN

The ephod was layered on top of the robe. Notice that the robe was called "the robe of the ephod" (Exodus 28:31). The robe was the setting for the ephod. The layers we have looked at so far are the tunic and the robe — the tunic represents the sinless humanity of Jesus, and the robe represents divinity of Jesus. This layered picture sets the stage for the ephod, the most elaborate and visible of the High Priest's garments. The ephod was an apron-like garment that was worn on top of the robe. It was of two pieces — front and back — held together at the shoulders by gold rings in which onyx stones were set. It was held to the priest's body by a girdle (wide belt) made to match the ephod itself. Tradition says that it reached to the knees in front, and to the ankles in back, though that is not specified in Scripture.

The ephod was made of linen, like the other garments. However, it was an intricately woven design of gold, blue, purples, and scarlet, with the gold listed first.

The gold—His pure, indestructible, divine, eternal life—is woven throughout the ephod, intermixed with the blue (divinity), purple (divinity and humanity combined: mediator), and the scarlet (humanity). The gold was not simply the color of gold, but gold cut into strands and woven through.

"They made the ephod of gold, and of blue, purple and scarlet yarn, and of finely twisted linen. They hammered out thin sheets of gold and cut strands to be worked into the blue, purple and scarlet yarn and fine linen—the work of skilled hands" (Exodus 39:2–3).

The gold added to the three colors of our Savior and the salvation He secured, brings into the mix the Eternal Spirit. Henry W. Saltau explains, in *The Tabernacle, the Priesthood, and the Offerings*, "Thus, the strength and glory of the gold was intimately blended with every part of the ephod, and gave firmness, as well as brilliancy, to the whole fabric."

This is the life of Jesus in heaven, administered by His Spirit on earth. In the "days of his flesh," He allowed Himself to be made in the likeness of frail flesh so that He could die; He partook of flesh and blood so that He could offer it up. Now, that very Savior is resurrected and at the right hand of the Father. His resurrection life blends it all together into one covering, beautiful, glorious garment. We are clothed in His power from on high.

We saw in the blue robe of the ephod that heaven was brought to earth when Jesus left heaven's throne room to be born of a virgin. He lived out His earthly life in the power of heaven. He brought heaven into earth. When He ascended, He brought earth into heaven. Jesus is where heaven and earth meet.

The ephod was made of the same colors as the veil that hid the Holy of Holies from the Holy Place, or Sanctuary of the Tabernacle. The gold was not woven into the veil, but was hidden behind the veil in the Holy of Holies. Like the ephod was hung from the shoulders of the High Priest by golden settings, the Tabernacle veil was hung on gold hooks.

"Make a curtain of blue, purple and scarlet yarn and finely twisted linen, with cherubim woven into it by a skilled worker. Hang it with gold hooks on four posts of acacia wood overlaid with gold and standing on four silver bases. Hang the curtain from the clasps and place the ark of the covenant law behind the curtain. The curtain will separate the Holy Place from the Most Holy Place" (Exodus 26:31–33).

SEPARATED

The Hebrew word translated "veil" (*pārōket*) comes from the root word paras, which means "to divide or break in two." The third veil in the Tabernacle covered the Holy of Holies and separated man from the Shekinah Presence of God. The High Priest entered in once a year, on the Day of Atonement, but only through carefully prescribed ceremonies and offerings. Sinful mankind and holy God were "broken in two." The Scripture clearly indicates this veil to be representative of Jesus' flesh.

"Therefore, brethren, since we have confidence to enter the holy place by the blood of Jesus, by a new and living way which He inaugurated for us through the veil, that is, His flesh" (Hebrews 10:19–20 NASB; author's emphasis).

In His flesh, He was fully God (blue), fully man (scarlet), and so the Mediator (purple) of a new and better covenant. When His flesh was torn, the veil in the Temple was simultaneously torn in two from top to bottom. The veil was not eternal, so it had no gold in its design. Eternity lay beyond the veil. When the full work that secured our eternal life was finished, the veil was torn. The gold lay waiting.

"And when Jesus had cried out again in a loud voice, he gave up his spirit. At that moment the curtain of the temple was torn in two from top to bottom" (Matthew 27:50–51).

When Jesus Himself had poured out His blood as our atonement sacrifice and Great High Priest, that which was broken in two — mankind and God — were brought together in Him. The way that had been closed was now open. A new and living way into the very presence of God was torn open. It was not curtains parting, but a heavy, strong veil ripped so as never to be repaired. Nothing can reverse what Christ has accomplished.

—◊—

Review what you see in the ephod and the veil that divided the Holy of Holies from the Holy Place.

Why is there no gold in the veil?

What do you think it means that gold is added to the design of the ephod?

MADE ONE

The ephod shows us that we have moved from being "broken in two" and separated from the presence of God, to being at one with Him. Restored to the position that mankind had before his fall — when sin entered into his heart. Full access, intimacy, childlike trust.

Just as Adam and Eve became "one flesh," Paul says that when we unite with Jesus, we become one Spirit with Him. "But whoever is united with the Lord is one with him in spirit" (1 Corinthians 6:17). Jesus has brought heaven into earth and earth into heaven. By His Spirit, heaven invades earth. By His ascension and His position at the right hand of the Father, earth has access to heaven.

The heavenly realms and the earthly realm were divided so completely that the Scripture refers to a gap between heaven and earth. The blue of Jesus' divinity and the scarlet of His humanity brought the two widely separated ends of the continuum together. Now, heaven is more than a place where we go when we die. Heaven — the spiritual aspects of reality — are part of our present experience. Heaven and earth are in a continual interaction. Earth's needs are brought to heaven's throne, and heaven's power is released in earth's circumstances.

DAY 2

MANNA: SUBSTANCE FROM HEAVEN

In John 6:35, Jesus made the claim "I am the bread of life." The audience who heard Him in real time did not hear "bread," but "manna." They had been in a discussion about the manna God had provided for Moses and the Israelites in the desert, and in the course of that discussion Jesus said, "I am the Manna that lives."

Let's think for a minute about manna. Remember that it was provided one day at a time, morning by morning, just enough for the day. When the Israelites went to bed at night, there was no sign of manna. No hint of its existence. But when they woke up in the morning, there it was. Question: where was the manna when it was not visible? It was in the heavenly realms. It was, the rabbis said, "The bread that came from heaven." The night before it was in the heavenly realms and not visible from earth, but the next morning, that which existed in the heavenly realms had moved into the environment of earth.

When Jesus claimed to be Living Manna, He was claiming that which was in the spiritual realms had moved into the environment of earth. He was saying, "I have brought heaven into earth." When He ascended and returned in the form of His Spirit, as He promised He would, the substance of heaven came to reside forever in the environment of earth. He brought heaven with Him when He came in the power of His Spirit.

POWER FROM ON HIGH

Settle in on this phrase that describes the Holy Spirit: "power from on high." I know we have used it throughout the study, but let's stop and really let it get a foothold in our hearts and minds.

What does that phrase say to you, "Power from on high."

When the Holy Spirit enters your life at salvation, He brings with Him the power that heaven has but earth does not. He brings something entirely new. Something we can't experience apart from Him. He brings heaven with Him.

We are still in our biological flesh, so heaven's power and presence can't all fit just right. Jesus, through His Spirit, is operating in us, through us, for us, but still limited by the confines of earth and flesh. His presence working in us begins to open up and push back those confines. The power that comes from on high works in us to enlarge the boundaries of what is possible.

Remember that, during Jesus' walk on earth, the Holy Spirit was working in and through His biological flesh. The Spirit empowers and equips us to do and think way past our natural abilities. More than simply making the old "me" better and stronger, He is creating a new "me." The old me is gone and the new me—the one with power from on high — is born. The new me has all of the physical characteristics of the old me, and even some of the same habits and thoughts of the old me, but where I used to be powered by the best I can do, now I'm powered by the best He can do.

ON DEPOSIT

The Scripture calls it a down payment, or deposit.

—ᴧᴧ—

Look at the following declarations about the Holy Spirit and identify what the Spirit is saying to you about His presence in your life.

"When you believed, you were marked in him with a seal, the promised Holy Spirit, who is a deposit guaranteeing our inheritance until the redemption of those who are God's possession — to the praise of his glory" (Ephesians 1:13–14).

"Now the one who has fashioned us for this very purpose is God, who has given us the Spirit as a deposit, guaranteeing what is to come" (2 Corinthians 5:5).

"He anointed us, set his seal of ownership on us, and put his Spirit in our hearts as a deposit, guaranteeing what is to come" (2 Corinthians 1:22).

—⟡—

What we can experience of His Spirit right now is beyond what we can imagine, but is still only a drop in the bucket of what is available. The more we allow the Spirit to fill us and change us, the more of Him we can experience. No matter how much of Him we know on earth, the full force of the Spirit is beyond our comprehension. But He is our inheritance. The full and complete power of His Spirit unbound by any flesh. As we learn to walk in His power and provision more each day, we also learn to long for Him more.

When I let the whole Scripture speak with His one voice, here is what I believe He teaches us.

1. The Holy Spirit comes to us at salvation. He is how we are moved out of the kingdom of darkness and into the kingdom of the Son He loves. (See Colossians 1:13.)

2. All of the Holy Spirit comes to indwell us because He is not a substance that can be watered down or divided up, but is God. (See 1 John 2:20.)

3. We don't experience all of Him at once because we are still in our human nature and our biological flesh. All of the Spirit is in us, but not all of the Spirit is on us. The Scripture describes an anointing that is in us (see 1 John 2:27).

4. As the Spirit who is in us gets access to our emotions, our minds, and our wills, then He begins to work through us so that He is not only in us, but on us. He shows. We are His witnesses — we stand as evidence that He is real and is in residence. He begins to saturate our lives.

5. We can grieve Him, or quench Him, or we can release Him — unleash Him to work freely and fully. We can let Him flow, baptizing every aspect of our lives and personalities in Him. We can resist, or we can yield.

The substance of heaven — the power from on high — is a Person. The Spirit of Christ. The Holy Spirit. He is there for you right now with heaven's resources. Everything heaven's got flows through Him and He is in you. Unleash Him to work freely and fully.

MORE!

Are you amazed that God wants to show you more of heaven's power day by day until the day we shed these earthly frames and experience Him unveiled and in the full force of His glory?

Every moment we live, we have the opportunity to give the Spirit more control of our lives; to see Him do in us, for us, and through us more than we can ask or even imagine. He is like rushing water, ready to fill any space left open to Him. He is forceful enough to flush out impediments in His way, and to change the inner landscape of the life left open to Him.

When the Scripture promises the Spirit like rivers of living water flowing from our inmost being, the Scripture is describing the spiritual, eternal picture of life-giving water that gushed from the rock in the desert (1 Corinthians 10:4). Let's consider the story.

In the midst of a desert, where no water source could be found, the Lord caused water to gush from a rock (see Numbers 20:11). Enough water so that the whole nation of Israel and all their livestock drank all they needed. Rivers of water poured forth. An unending supply. Enough to "turn the desert into pools of water, and the parched ground into springs" (Isaiah 41:18).

The Holy Spirit is the Power from on High. We can have all of Him we make room for in our lives, but there will still be more. My first waking prayer in recent years is, "More!"

DAY 3

The ephod reminds us that heaven and earth are no longer curtained off from each other, but instead heaven has opened the way for the two to become one. Though we live on earth in time and space, we have access to heaven's realms. Heaven and earth are one place. We live on earth, supplied by heaven. We walk on earth, led by heaven.

"For God was pleased to have all his fullness dwell in him, and through him to reconcile to himself all things, whether things on earth or things in heaven, by making peace through his blood, shed on the cross (Colossians 1:19–20).

"With all wisdom and understanding, he made known to us the mystery of his will according to his good pleasure, which he purposed in Christ, to be put into effect when the times reach their fulfillment — to bring unity to all things in heaven and on earth under Christ" (Ephesians 1:8–10).

Immersed into the realms of the Spirit, we find that the spiritual realm is not ethereal and insubstantial. Rather, the spiritual realm is where the power is. The power of the spiritual realm acts on the material realm. The material realm is reactive and temporary, while the spiritual realm is causative and eternal.

INVISIBLE POWER, VISIBLE RESULTS

The realities of the spiritual realm are invisible, but that does not make them less real.

"For since the creation of the world God's invisible qualities — his eternal power and divine nature — have been clearly seen, being understood from what has been made, so that people are without excuse" (Romans 1:20; author's emphasis).

In fact, most of our universe is invisible, according to science. Paul says that creation included visible and invisible elements.

"For in him all things were created: things in heaven and on earth, visible and invisible, whether thrones or powers or rulers or authorities; all things have been created through him and for him" (Colossians 1:16).

I explored this in my book *Fueled by Faith:*

> Most of the universe is invisible. So say those who study it closely. Those who put it under powerful microscopes and examine it from every vantage point. Most of creation is invisible. They refer to "dark matter" and "dark energy," by which they mean energy and substance that are hidden from view. This dark matter and dark energy must exist, but we just can't see them.
>
> Neutrinos, for example (particles too small to be seen or measured). "Neutrinos, unseen and beyond counting, fill the universe. People call them ghostly, but ghosts aren't real. Neutrinos are real. . . ." No one has ever seen one, but the effect they produce prove their existences. Stranger still, ". . . it seems that a given neutrino does not have one stable mass or one stable

identity. Instead, as it flies along, it oscillates from one identity—what physicists call a flavor, which means a way of interacting with other particles—to another." Neutrinos, which no one has ever seen, are so numerous that ". . . if they have even a tiny mass, they outweigh all the stars and galaxies, all the visible matter in the universe. They might make up as much as one fifth of the dark matter that physicists and astrophysicists have been seeking so assiduously." (Discover, August 2001, "The Unbearably Unstoppable Neutrino" by Rober Kunzig)

Now think about this. The most fact-based, pragmatic, proof-demanding physicists say that most of the universe is invisible. They don't claim that it doesn't exist, just that it is invisible. So if you look at the air and it looks empty, it's not. That is an illusion. In fact, there is no such thing as "emptiness."

What if the spiritual realm, which we might tend to think of as "a galaxy far, far away," to borrow a phrase from Star Wars, is really not far, far away. What if it is really all around you.. What if, something like all that dark energy and dark mass, the spiritual realm is operating in direct interaction with the material realm. Jesus said, "Repent, for the kingdom of heaven is near" (Matt. 4:17), "Repent"—change your mind. But more than just change your opinion, it means think differently. It means reorient your mind. Set it differently. Tune your thoughts to a different dimension. Why? Because the kingdom of heaven is "near," or the King James Version says "at hand." The Greek word means that it is squeezing you, pressing in on you. At hand—reach out your hand and there it *is. I have often thought about how easily Jesus moved back and forth between time and eternity—between material and physical—during the forty days when He appeared on earth after His resurrection and before His ascension. He was in the spiritual realm, invisible, and the next moment He was in the material realm. I don't think He was traveling back and forth between two widely separated locations, do you? The molecular structure of His body just changed to accommodate one realm or the other. When He is invisible, He is still present.*

Now, I know that the Kingdom of God is within us, but I think it is of such a composition that it is in us and around us and through us and between us. Neutrinos are constantly traveling through us. In one side and out the other. If neutrinos can be around us and in us and through us, surely so can the Kingdom.

Whatever the explanation, the spiritual realm is present and active in our lives. It is not a different location, but a different dimension. It is real and solid and available every moment.

—∾∾—

Underline or highlight the phrases that tell you earth and heaven interact.

"And God raised us up with Christ and seated us with him in the heavenly realms in Christ Jesus" (Ephesians 2:6).

"Since, then, you have been raised with Christ, set your hearts on things above, where Christ is, seated at the right hand of God. Set your minds on things above, not on earthly things. For you died, and your life is now hidden with Christ in God" (Colossians 3:1–3).

How would it change your perspective if you believed that the Spirit and the heavenly realms were real, substantial, and at hand?

DAY 4

"They made shoulder pieces for the ephod, which were attached to two of its corners, so it could be fastened. . . . They mounted the onyx stones in gold filigree settings and engraved them like a seal with the names of the sons of Israel. Then they fastened them on the shoulder pieces of the ephod as memorial stones for the sons of Israel, as the LORD *commanded Moses"* (Exodus 39:4, 6–7).

The ephod was made of two pieces — front and back. Those two pieces were connected and made into one garment at the shoulders. At the shoulders, the two pieces were fastened by settings of gold filigree into which was mounted an onyx stone. One stone was on each shoulder. The stones bore the names of the sons of Israel, or the 12 tribes, 6 names on each. Each tribe represented every person in that tribe. On the shoulders of the high priest were the people. All believers were represented in those 12 tribes.

"Take two onyx stones and engrave on them the names of the sons of Israel in the order of their birth — six names on one stone and the remaining six on the other. Engrave the names of the sons of Israel on the two stones the way a gem cutter engraves a seal. Then mount the stones in gold filigree settings and fasten them on the shoulder pieces of the ephod as memorial stones for the sons of Israel. Aaron is to bear the names on his shoulders as a memorial before the LORD. *Make gold filigree settings and two braided chains of pure gold, like a rope, and attach the chains to the settings"* (Exodus 28:9–14).

Notice how very specific the instructions are about how the names are to be engraved. They are not to be tattooed on, or written on, but engraved "the way a gem cutter engraves a seal." The names will become one with the stone. They cannot be removed from the stone.

Just as when He engraves us on the palm of His hand:

"See, I have engraved you on the palms of my hands" (Isaiah 49:16). No one, nothing, can ever remove us from His hands.

"I give them eternal life, and they shall never perish; no one will snatch them out of my hand. My Father, who has given them to me, is greater than all; no one can snatch them out of my Father's hand. I and the Father are one" (John 10:28–30).

Jesus is our High Priest who carries us on His shoulders — the place of His strength. He is the onyx stone into which we have been graven forever. He is the gold filigree that holds the two pieces together. By His Spirit, He carries us in His strength, on His shoulders. "Not by might nor by power, but by my Spirit,' says the LORD Almighty" (Zechariah 4:6). Jesus can't be summed up in a single metaphor. It takes a slew of pictures and illustrations to show us His role in our lives and how His Spirit displays Him to us.

Moses, as the people of Israel came to the edge of the Promised Land and trembled at the enemy they saw, said:

"Do not be terrified; do not be afraid of them. The LORD your God, who is going before you, will fight for you, as he did for you in Egypt, before your very eyes, and in the wilderness. There you saw how the LORD your God carried you, as a father carries his son, all the way you went until you reached this place" (Deuteronomy 1:29–31).

He carries us on His shoulders, like a man carries a son. Our weakness leans into His strength. We can rest in His love for us because we are ever on His shoulders. The Holy Spirit makes this truth real and present to us. We can carry each others' burdens because we are carried on His shoulders, in the power of His Spirit.

"Now we who are strong ought to bear the weaknesses of those without strength and not just please ourselves. Each of us is to please his neighbor for his good, to his edification" (Romans 15:1–2 NASB).

When the strength of His Spirit causes us to be carried on His shoulders, then we have the strength to bear each others' burdens. When we bear a burden, we bear it to Him and leave it there.

—ᴧᴧ—

Right now, let the Spirit show you your name engraved on the Onyx Stone. With the eyes of your heart, see it. Your name. Your life. Your weakness. Carried on His shoulders.

Speak aloud the places in your life right now that you are resting on His strength.

Let His power clothe you, rest on you, and feel the burdens transfer from your shoulders to His. Let the Spirit lift each burden as it comes to mind and place each on the strong shoulders of Jesus. List the burdens you have transferred to Him.

—ᴧᴧ—

The ephod was held to the High Priest by a waistband or girdle made of the same materials so that there is no separation between the ephod and the sash.

"Its skillfully woven waistband was like it — of one piece with the ephod and made with gold, and with blue, purple and scarlet yarn, and with finely twisted linen, as the LORD commanded Moses" (Exodus 39:5).

Henry W. Soltau says that the purpose of the sash or the waistband was to so connect the ephod with the person who wore it, as to impart to him the virtues it contained. The Spirit who has clothed you in the heavenly ephod — bringing heaven and earth together and imparting strength — fastens Himself to you. Not loosely, but binds Himself around you, holding His anointing in place. Perhaps this is to picture Him with arms wrapped tightly around you, securing you in His strength.

DAY 5

"Fashion a breastpiece for making decisions — the work of skilled hands. Make it like the ephod: of gold, and of blue, purple and scarlet yarn, and of finely twisted linen. It is to be square — a span long and a span wide — and folded double. Then mount four rows of precious stones on it. . . . Mount them in gold filigree settings. There are to be twelve stones, one for each of the names of the sons of Israel, each engraved like a seal with the name of one of the twelve tribes.

"For the breastpiece make braided chains of pure gold, like a rope. Make two gold rings for it and fasten them to two corners of the breastpiece. Fasten the two gold chains to the rings at the corners of the breastpiece, and the other ends of the chains to the two settings, attaching them to the shoulder pieces of the ephod at the front. Make two gold rings and attach them to the other two corners of the breastpiece on the inside edge next to the ephod. Make two more gold rings and attach them to the bottom of the shoulder pieces on the front of the ephod, close to the

seam just above the waistband of the ephod. The rings of the breastpiece are to be tied to the rings of the ephod with blue cord, connecting it to the waistband, so that the breastpiece will not swing out from the ephod.

"Whenever Aaron enters the Holy Place, he will bear the names of the sons of Israel over his heart on the breastpiece of decision as a continuing memorial before the LORD. *Also put the Urim and the Thummim in the breastpiece, so they may be over Aaron's heart whenever he enters the presence of the* LORD. *Thus Aaron will always bear the means of making decisions for the Israelites over his heart before the* LORD*"* (Exodus 28:15–30).

The final portion of the ephod is the breastpiece. It is made of the same materials as the ephod and is connected to the ephod by gold chains attached to the shoulder settings. Remember that the shoulder settings signify that we are carried in His strength. On the breastpiece, we are carried on His heart. His love for us is connected to His strength. He loves us with all His strength.

Let's look at the details of the breastpiece and glean what the Spirit is teaching about Himself.

DECISION MAKER

First, it is called "a breastpiece for making decisions." Some translations translate it "breastpiece of judgment." This judgment does not mean passing judgment on right or wrong, but instead means governing, or making decisions. The primary definition of the breastpiece, then, is for making decisions.

This was accomplished through the Urim and the Thummim, mysterious stones that were to be kept in the breastpiece, which was folded over to make something like a pocket. The Urim and the Thummin were to be over Aaron's heart whenever he went before the Lord so that the Lord could tell the people, through Aaron, what His will was in any given matter.

The pocket of the breastpiece and the Urim and the Thummin tell us of the Holy Spirit's ability to reveal the will of God at any given moment. In the Old Testament, when the Spirit was not indwelling the people, using a form of casting lots—as God directed—was a common way for God to reveal His specific will in a specific situation. "The lot is cast into the lap, but its every decision is from the LORD" (Proverbs 16:33).

No one is clear on exactly how the Urim and the Thummin were employed, but they in some way similar to casting lots revealed God's answers. We no longer need any such methods because we have been clothed with His power from on high and He can reveal the Lord's mind to us.

—◊◊◊—

Underline or highlight phrases that tell you wisdom (discernment) comes from the Holy Spirit.

"We continually ask God to fill you with the knowledge of his will through all the wisdom and understanding that the Spirit gives" (Colossians 1:9).

"My goal is that they may be encouraged in heart and united in love, so that they may have the full riches of complete understanding, in order that they may know the mystery of God, namely, Christ, in whom are hidden all the treasures of wisdom and knowledge" (Colossians 2:2–3).

Remember that Christ is full of the Spirit and you are full of Christ.

"If any of you lacks wisdom, you should ask God, who gives generously to all without finding fault, and it will be given to you" (James 1:5).

—◊◊◊—

The Holy Spirit can speak the mind of Jesus directly to you. He can speak so intimately that He makes direct deposits from His mind to yours. His voice is closer than words spoken from another's mouth to your ears. When Jesus told His disciples that He would go away so the Spirit could come, He did not say that speaking from within would be less effective than His physical presence with them. Just the opposite.

"But very truly I tell you, it is for your good that I am going away. Unless I go away, the Advocate will not come to you; but if I go, I will send him to you" (John 16:7).

The indwelling Holy Spirit is not second best. He has always been the ultimate plan, the culmination of the plan. The way the Holy Spirit can speak to us is easier for us to hear than if Jesus were standing in His physical form speaking audible words to your ears.

—ɯ—

In the following recorded incidents, underline or highlight the words and phrases that indicate that the Holy Spirit can speak present tense to believers.

"While they were worshiping the Lord and fasting, the Holy Spirit said" (Acts 13:2).

"Then Saul, who was also called Paul, filled with the Holy Spirit, looked straight at Elymas and said, 'You are a child of the devil and an enemy of everything that is right' (Acts 13:9–10).

"The Spirit told Philip, 'Go to that chariot and stay near it'" (Acts 8:29).

"While Peter was still thinking about the vision, the Spirit said to him, 'Simon, three men are looking for you. So get up and go downstairs. Do not hesitate to go with them, for I have sent them'" (Acts 10:19).

What do you need God's wisdom on right now? Write it down here, and date it. Trust that the Lord will reveal His mind through His Spirit in you.

OVER HIS HEART

The breastpiece had 12 stones, each one engraved with a name of one of the tribes of Israel. Again, each name represented each person of that tribe, and all tribes were represented. On the shoulders, all the names were engraved on the same kind of stone — onyx. On the breastpiece, each name was engraved on a different stone, each stone precious. Each stone reflected the light differently. Each as beautiful as another, but different. The breastpiece, and the precious stones set into the breastpiece by gold, were all one garment.

The Holy Spirit distributes His gifts to each of us individually. Those gifts are different, and reflect the Lord differently, but each is beautiful. The purpose of these gifts is to build up the body and to glorify God. The gold filigree that held the stones in place on the breastpiece pictures the eternal Spirit in whom we become one with each other, as we become one with Christ.

—⚶—

How do each of these passages give a picture of the breastpiece?

"For just as each of us has one body with many members, and these members do not all have the same function, so in Christ we, though

many, form one body, and each member belongs to all the others.
We have different gifts, according to the grace given to each of us"
(Romans 12:4–6).

"There are different kinds of gifts, but the same Spirit distributes
them. There are different kinds of service, but the same Lord. There
are different kinds of working, but in all of them and in everyone it
is the same God at work.

Now to each one the manifestation of the Spirit is given for
the common good. . . . All these are the work of one and the same
Spirit, and he distributes them to each one, just as he determines"
(1 Corinthians 12:4–11).

—ᴍ—

You are a precious stone on the breastpiece of your Great High Priest, who carries your name on His heart before the Father always. Just as you are dressed in Him, He is dressed in you. You are His adornment. By His Spirit, you sparkle. He polishes you, and sets you in a golden setting, and wears you with pleasure.

WEEK SIX

 HEAVENLY MINDED

"But you have an anointing from the Holy One, and all of you know the truth. As for you, the anointing you received from him remains in you, and you do not need anyone to teach you. But as his anointing teaches you about all things and as that anointing is real, not counterfeit —just as it has taught you, remain in him" (1 John 2:20–27).

DAY 1

"Make the turban of fine linen" (Exodus 28:39).

The only thing we know about the turban is that it was made of fine white linen and that it covered the priest's head. I think that speaks for itself. Righteousness covering the mind, the seat of all our thoughts and understanding. Jesus said that He would teach deeper truths through His Spirit.

"I have much more to say to you, more than you can now bear. But when he, the Spirit of truth, comes, he will guide you into all the truth. He will not speak on his own; he will speak only what he hears, and he will tell you what is yet to come" (John 16:12–13).

Jesus was speaking to the disciples with whom He had spent three intense years. He had kept them near Him, teaching them both by word and example. He had imparted to them everything it was possible for them to absorb. But He had more to teach them. He had truth to reveal to them that was too deep for them to receive in their natural state. Just think. Jesus had truth to reveal that was of such depth that He could only reveal it from inside them.

He referred to the coming Spirit as the Spirit of truth. The word translated "truth" means a reality that is to be regarded as firm and reliable. The Holy Spirit will guide us into all truth. He will illumine our minds so that we can ascertain truth.

Paul calls Him "the Spirit of wisdom and revelation."

—ɯ—

Use this passage to answer the questions that follow.

"I keep asking that the God of our Lord Jesus Christ, the glorious Father, may give you the Spirit of wisdom and revelation, so that you may know him better. I pray that the eyes of your heart may be enlightened in order that you may know the hope to which he has called you, the riches of his glorious inheritance in his holy people, and his incomparably great power for us who believe" (Ephesians 1:17-19).

What do you think it means that the Holy Spirit is the Spirit of wisdom and revelation?

Is there knowledge and understanding that are beyond our natural ability to grasp, but that we can receive from the Spirit?

Notice the passive tense of the verb when Paul prays that "the eyes of your heart may be enlightened." That means someone else does the enlightening and you receive the enlightening. What do you think Paul means by "the eyes of your heart"? Who does the enlightening?

When the eyes of your heart are enlightened, you will know (comprehend, apprehend) what three things?

Look at the next part of the passage, then answer the questions that follow.

"That power is the same as the mighty strength he exerted when he raised Christ from the dead and seated him at his right hand in the heavenly realms, far above all rule and authority, power and dominion, and every name that is invoked, not only in the present age but also in the one to come. And God placed all things under his feet and appointed him to be head over everything for the church, which is his body, the fullness of him who fills everything in every way" (Ephesians 1:19–23).

When the Spirit of wisdom and revelation enlightens your inner eyes so you can comprehend deep truths, one thing revealed is "the incomparably great power of God for us who believe." Now Paul is about to define that power. The first thing about the power available to us is that it is "the same as the mighty strength he exerted when he _____ from the dead." What does that say to you about the power His Spirit reveals?

The next thing Paul says about the power available is "and seated him at his right hand in the _____ ,
far above all _____ ."
What does that tell you about God's power revealed to you by His Spirit?

Andrew Murray says, "Not from without but from within, not in word but in power, in lifeand truth, the Spirit reveals Christ and all He has for us. He makes the Christ, who has been to us so much only an image, a thought, a Saviour outside and above us, to be truth within us. The Spirit brings the truth into us; and then, having possessed us from within, guides us, as we can bear it, into all the truth." (*The Spirit of Christ*)

UNVEILED

As the Holy Spirit covers you, He works in your mind and understanding to progressively reveal the deep and hidden things.

"He reveals deep and hidden things;
he knows what lies in darkness,
and light dwells with him" (Daniel 2:22).

The word *reveal* means unveiling or uncovering. It is the word the Scripture uses over and over to describe how the Holy Spirit teaches us unknowable truth. He pulls the covering off what? Our minds.

"But their minds were made dull, for to this day the same veil remains when the old covenant is read. It has not been removed, because only in Christ is it taken away. Even to this day when Moses is read, a veil covers their hearts. But whenever anyone turns to the Lord, the veil is taken away" (2 Corinthians 3:14–16).

The Holy Spirit pulls back the veil over our understanding that prevents us from seeing the full light of all truth. Every time we understand a spiritual truth it is because the Holy Spirit has pulled back the veil and shown us what lies beneath the surface. When God speaks to you from within, He is acting directly on your understanding. The word Scripture uses to describe the direct action of God on your mind and understanding is *revelation.*

DAY 2

John tells us that the Holy Spirit in us reveals all truth to us.

"But you have an anointing from the Holy One, and all of you know the truth. As for you, the anointing you received from him remains in you, and you do not need anyone to teach you. But as his anointing teaches you about all things and as that anointing is real, not counterfeit — just as it has taught you, remain in him" (1 John 2:20–27).

The anointing is always a reference to the Holy Spirit. We have the Holy Spirit as an anointing in us, flowing through every part of our minds. When John says that we know all truth, He doesn't mean that we are all-knowing and need no teaching or instruction. He means that the truth is living in us as the eternal Spirit, and that, when we recognize truth, it has come from Him and is revealed from within. He means that there is no truth that is not available to you from the Spirit as you need it, and as you can receive it.

THE TRUTH TELLER

God speaks by revealing the truth in His Word at progressively deeper levels. Only He can do that. No matter how wonderful you may think a speaker or writer is, he or she cannot reveal truth to your understanding. If someone's words have produced new insight in you, it is because God Himself has revealed it. Information comes from outside sources. Revelation comes from God within you.

First Corinthians 2:9–16 shows the difference between information about God and revelation from God.

"No eye has seen, no ear has heard, no mind has conceived what God has prepared for those who love him" (v. 9).

God has things prepared for us — things that are ready and waiting for our use. We cannot know these things in the same way we know what exists on the earth. We can't know God's provision by seeing or hearing or imagining.

"But God has revealed it to us by his Spirit" (v. 10).

What we cannot know by seeing, hearing, or imagining, we can know by the Spirit's revelation. The Spirit unveils God's truths to our understanding. When the Spirit brings understanding, we will know what God has ready and waiting as certainly as if we'd seen them with our eyes or heard them with our ears.

"The Spirit searches all things, even the deep things of God" (v. 10).

When we are depending on the Spirit to bring understanding of spiritual truth, we will have access to even the deep, mysterious, hidden things that belong to God. See Daniel 2:22.

"For who among men knows the thoughts of a man except the man's spirit within him?" (v. 11).

No one knows me but me. No one knows my thoughts but my spirit within me. If you want to know what I think, I will have to reveal my thoughts to you.

In the same way, no one knows the thoughts of God except the Spirit of God (v. 11).

Just like no one knows me but me, no one knows God but God. If you want to know His thoughts, He will have to reveal them to you.

We have not received the spirit of the world but the Spirit who is from God, that we may understand what God has freely given us (v. 12).

God has revealed Himself to us. He has given us His Spirit. He has given us Himself. The purpose for giving us His Spirit is so that we can understand what He has prepared for us and has made freely available to us.

"This is what we speak, not in words taught us by human wisdom but in words taught by the Spirit, expressing spiritual truths in spiritual words," (v. 13).

What do we speak? We speak what we understand. What does God's Spirit cause us to understand? From the Spirit, we understand what God has freely given us. If God Himself has revealed truth into our understanding, when we. speak that understanding, we are speaking spiritual words. What makes them.spiritual? They are born of the Spirit. Whatever is born of the Spirit is spirit. We can now say, "These words I speak, they are spirit and they are life."

What is your response to realizing that your mind is covered and anointed by the Holy Spirit?

MINDFUL LIVING

Spiritual battles are fought in the mind. In your mind, you embrace either lies or truth. Once you align your thinking with either the enemy's lie or the Spirit's truth, then your course is set.

The Person who is truth lives in you. He has direct access to your mind and thoughts. He can always reveal truth to you in any moment. He can do a truth download. You just have to make yourself available.

The Scripture instructs us to "set our minds" (Colossians 3:2). Take a deliberate and determined action to put your mind on things above because though you live on earth, you live by heaven's power. The Holy Spirit has direct access to your mind and thoughts and you can choose to let Him redirect your thoughts, guiding you into all truth. "We have the mind of Christ" (1 Corinthians 2:16).

"Since, then, you have been raised with Christ, set your hearts on things above, where Christ is, seated at the right hand of God. Set your minds on things above, not on earthly things. For you died, and your life is now hidden with Christ in God. When Christ, who is your life, appears, then you also will appear with him in glory" (Colossians 3:1–4).

Your emotions, your decisions, your responses and reactions, everything about living your life flows from your mind, which in Scripture is often translated "heart."

"Above all else, guard your heart, for everything you do flows from it" (Proverbs 4:23).

Your mind is where every action, every word, every emotion has its beginning. You can't think one way and be another, at least not for the long haul. You may pull it off short term, but in the end what you think is who you are becoming.

"A good man brings good things out of the good stored up in his heart, and an evil man brings evil things out of the evil stored up in his heart. For the mouth speaks what the heart is full of" (Luke 6:45).

—⁓—

Consider these words that Jesus spoke, and then answer questions following.

"Make a tree good and its fruit will be good, or make a tree bad and its fruit will be bad, for a tree is recognized by its fruit. You brood of vipers, how can you who are evil say anything good? For the mouth speaks what the heart is full of. A good man brings good things out of the good stored up in him, and an evil man brings evil things out of the evil stored up in him. But I tell you that everyone will have to give account on the day of judgment for every empty word they have spoken. For by your words you will be acquitted, and by your words you will be condemned."

How do you understand Jesus to be comparing tree and fruit to thoughts and words?

What do words reveal about your spiritual condition?

Is the problem the words per se, or what the words reveal?

—ɯ—

The mind is where thoughts are nurtured and fed, or rejected and replaced. The Holy Spirit covers your mind with His presence, infuses your mind with His truth.

"Do not conform to the pattern of this world, but be transformed by the renewing of your mind. Then you will be able to test and approve what God's will is — his good, pleasing and perfect will" (Romans 12:2).

"Be made new in the attitude of your minds; and to put on the new self, created to be like God in true righteousness and holiness" (Ephesians 4:23–24).

Our part is to surrender to His power and deliberately set our minds. We put our minds in position to cooperate with Him. The renewing and restoring that He sets about at His first access to us happens in our minds.

"Those who live according to the flesh have their minds set on what the flesh desires; but those who live in accordance with the Spirit have their minds set on what the Spirit desires. The mind governed by the flesh is death, but the mind governed by the Spirit is life and peace. The mind governed by the flesh is hostile to God; it does not submit to God's law, nor can it do so. Those who are in the realm of the flesh cannot please God. You, however, are not in the realm of the flesh but are in the realm of the Spirit, if indeed the Spirit of God lives in you" (Romans 8:5–7; author's emphasis).

The Holy Spirit will lead you into all truth. When you were baptized by Him, He covered every wound, every memory, every lie, every misdirection. Yield to Him and let His mind flow through you. Deliberately, determinedly, purposefully replace lies that circulate in your thoughts with His truth.

—〰—

In Ephesians 3, Paul instructs us to set our minds on things above instead of setting our minds on things of earth. Like tuning a radio dial, attune your mind so that it is positioned to hear His truth. Then Paul goes on to give specifics about setting your mind. In the course of this passage he says the following. Read through this and see what words and visuals echo back to being clothed in priests' garments. What does this tell you about setting your mind?

"Therefore, as God's chosen people, holy and dearly loved, clothe yourselves with compassion, kindness, humility, gentleness and patience. Bear with each other and forgive one another if any of you has a grievance against someone. Forgive as the Lord forgave you. And over all these virtues put on love, which binds them all together in perfect unity" (Colossians 3:12–14).

DAY 3

We are getting the faintest glimpse of how the gift of His Spirit is designed to impact, change, and renew every detail of our lives. The One who created us in the beginning devised a salvation that would save every part of us.

"He holds his priesthood permanently, because he continues forever. Consequently, he is able to save to the uttermost [in all ways an at all times] those who draw near to God through him, since he always lives to make intercession for them" (Hebrews 7:24–25 ESV).

The fact that He is making intercession means more than simply saying prayers, but rather that He is a living prayer before God on our behalf. Jesus is the Praying Life.

He is everything to us. "It is because of him that you are in Christ Jesus, who has become for us wisdom from God—that is, our righteousness [white linen tunic], holiness [robe] and redemption [ephod]. Therefore, as it is written: 'Let the one who boasts boast in the Lord'" (1 Corinthians 1:30–31; bracketed words author's).

ALL OF HIM IN ALL OF ME

In the priests' garments so far, do you see that He loves you with all His heart (breastpiece), all His strength (shoulder clasps), and all his mind (turban)? When He invites us to love Him fully with all of who we are, He is asking us to love Him back in the same love with which He loves us. "This is love: not that we loved God, but that he loved us and sent his Son as an atoning sacrifice for our sins" (1 John 4:10–11).

In configuring our salvation, the Father took into account every aspect of our humanity that sin had wrecked and misaligned, and He made a plan that would cover it all. The Son would die for our sins so we could be forgiven and restored. The Spirit would fill and baptize us with Himself so our unrighteousness could be cleansed.

—ᜃ—

Right now, what circumstance in your life, or inner struggle, or relationship needs to be surrendered to the flow of His Spirit, and the Power from on high?

Is there anything about this particular struggle of yours for which the Spirit's power is inadequate?

Let Him baptize you afresh right now and let your heart's eyes see your struggle immersed in His power from on high. Let Him baptize your mind, your emotions, your perceptions, your understanding, your strength.

—ɯ—

With the promise of the Spirit came the promise that "you will be my witnesses." The natural consequence of being baptized in His Spirit is that our lives become convincing evidence of His presence and power. We are changed.

—ɯ—

Identify words and phrases that indicate how the Holy Spirit changes us by His power and presence. Look for what part of you He is changing and notice the language that says He is doing the action, and you are receiving the action.

"Do not conform to the pattern of this world, but be transformed by the renewing of your mind. Then you will be able to test and approve what God's will is—his good, pleasing and perfect will" (Romans 12:2).

"Since you have taken off your old self with its practices and have put on the new self, which is being renewed in knowledge in the image of its Creator" (Colossians 3:10–11).

"God's love has been poured out into our hearts through the Holy Spirit, who has been given to us" (Romans 5:5).

"Now to him who is able to do immeasurably more than all we ask or imagine, according to his power that is at work within us, to him be glory in the church and in Christ Jesus throughout all generations, forever and ever! Amen." (Ephesians 3:20–21).

Who is "His power at work within us"?

"Equip you in every good thing to do His will, working in us that which is pleasing in His sight, through Jesus Christ, to whom be the glory forever and ever. Amen" (Hebrews 13:21).

Who brings equipping power from on high?

"It is God who works in you to will and to act in order to fulfill his good purpose" (Philippians 2:13).

—〰—

Our salvation is a full-spectrum salvation and the Holy Spirit delivers the reality of Jesus to every nook and cranny of our humanity. We just need to let Him flow.

DAY 4

"Make a plate of pure gold and engrave on it as on a seal: HOLY TO THE
LORD. *Fasten a blue cord to it to attach it to the turban; it is to be on the
front of the turban. It will be on Aaron's forehead, and he will bear the
guilt involved in the sacred gifts the Israelites consecrate, whatever their
gifts may be. It will be on Aaron's forehead continually so that they will
be acceptable to the* LORD" (Exodus 28:36–38).

The final piece of the High Priest's garments is the golden crown to be
on his forehead. This golden crown, engraved with the seal "Holy to
the Lord" is the covering that ties everything together. This is what each
garment has been saying. Holy to the Lord.

CROWN HIM

This crown belongs only to our Great High Priest, but as we clothe
ourselves in Him, it covers us also. The power from on high brings into
our lives power that (1) we do not possess; and that (2) exists only in
heaven. Nothing the Holy Spirit delivers to our lives is ours by right, but
only as a gracious undeserved gift.

God sees n on our foreheads a golden plate, shaped into a crown-
like appearance. It is made of pure gold, signifying incorruptible and
everlasting life. It is engraved with a seal. The words and the golden
plate are one with each other. Holy — set apart for God's service. It is
our crowning glory that we are His.

This crown is attached to the turban with a blue cord. White linen
turban (righteous humanity) crowned in gold (everlasting) engraved
as holy (set apart) and fastened to the white turban with a cord of
blue (divinity). It is to be on the front of the turban and at the head of
the garments. The first thing seen by God, and the first thing seen by
mankind.

Because of this crown, any taint in the gifts offered to the Lord will
be absorbed and covered by the presence of our Great High Priest.

We are never 100 percent pure in our motives or actions. Even this problem is dealt with in the way our salvation is designed to work.

The crown is on Aaron's forehead. The forehead in Scripture tends to illustrate the seat of the will.

"For I knew how stubborn you were;
your neck muscles were iron,
your forehead was bronze" (Isaiah 48:4).

"But the people of Israel are not willing to listen to you because they are not willing to listen to me, for all the Israelites are hardened and obstinate. But I will make you as unyielding and hardened as they are. I will make your forehead like the hardest stone, harder than flint" (Ezekiel 3:7–9).

On our forehead is written HOLY TO THE LORD. Across the place of our will, yieldedness is written large. It is to be what defines us before the Lord and before others. Front and center, the highlight of our garments of salvation.

—ww—

Highlight or underline the phrases that tell you that our Great High Priest lived His earthly life with Holy Unto the Lord engraved on His forehead.

"My food," said Jesus, *"is to do the will of him who sent me and to finish his work"* (John 4:34).

"By myself I can do nothing; I judge only as I hear, and my judgment is just, for I seek not to please myself but him who sent me" (John 5:30).

"Going a little farther, he fell with his face to the ground and prayed, 'My Father, if it is possible, may this cup be taken from me. Yet not as I will, but as you will'" (Matthew 26:39).

How is the Holy Spirit delivering the obedience of Jesus into your life?

—ɱ—

How counterintuitive that the crown we wear is surrender and yielding rather than our own personal status or power. What a mirror image of how our human nature on its own defines a crown. The Holy Spirit baptizes us with power from on high, and that power's crowning garment — its pinnacle — is absolute surrender. The will handed over and relinquished. Here is what HOLY TO THE LORD looks like in a life. Here is our crown:

"For I have come down from heaven not to do my will but to do the will of him who sent me" (John 6:38).

DAY 5

You've seen that you are washed and immersed in the Spirit through the *mikveh* of the Spirit (baptism of the Spirit). Every obscure, concealed, unseen aspect of your humanity has been submerged and soaked in Him. You've seen that you are clothed in Him. You have been given a covering that blankets every part of your personality. From head to toe, you are swathed in Him.

Now see that you are anointed with Him.

"After you put these clothes on your brother Aaron and his sons, anoint and ordain them. Consecrate them so they may serve me as priests" (Exodus 28:41).

The last step of the priest's investiture was the anointing. The anointing oil was poured over the clothing of the priest after he was baptized and clothed. The anointing oil soaked into the fabric and wafted from the priest's covering as the priest served before the Lord, and among the people. His every movement transmitted a sweet fragrance. The anointing happened once, in one action, then lasted for the life of the garment. The fragrance of the anointing grew stronger over time as the olive oil infused with pungent spices soaked in and became part of the fabric, and the odors matured and grew richer.

The anointing oil is a picture of the Holy Spirit, poured out in the lives of God's priestly tribe. The anointing oil poured *on* in the Old Testament is the picture of the Spirit poured *in*.

—Ⅲ—

Read 1 John 2:20, 27.

"But you have an anointing from the Holy One, and all of you know the truth. . . . As for you, the anointing you received from him remains in you, and you do not need anyone to teach you. But as his anointing teaches you about all things and as that anointing is real, not counterfeit—just as it has taught you, remain in him."

Underline in the passage or write out the phrases that answer these questions:

1. From whom does the anointing come?

2. Who is the Holy One? (See Luke 1:35; Mark 1:24)

3. Where does the anointing remain?

4. The anointing teaches you. Underline the phrases that indicate this.

5. Can an inanimate object teach you?

6. What shows you that the anointing is a person and not a thing?

7. From this passage, what does the Spirit (anointing) teach you?

Read John 14:26 and John 16:13.

"But the Advocate, the Holy Spirit, whom the Father will send in my name, will teach you all things and will remind you of everything I have said to you. . . . But when he, the Spirit of truth, comes, he will guide you into all the truth."

1. What will the Holy Spirit teach you?

2. Jesus calls the Holy Spirit "the Spirit of _____

_____ ."

3. In the passage from 1 John, what do you know because the Holy Spirit is in you? You know the _____

_____ ."

SATURATED

Jesus declared Himself anointed.

WEEK 6
DAY 5
153

The Spirit of the Lord is on me,
  because he has anointed me
  to proclaim good news to the poor.
He has sent me to proclaim freedom for the prisoners
  and recovery of sight for the blind,
to set the oppressed free,
  to proclaim the year of the Lord's favor (Luke 4:18–19).

After reading these words from the prophet Isaiah, Jesus proclaimed that Scripture fulfilled. He was the Anointed One. The Spirit of the Lord was on Him because the Spirit of the Lord was in Him. The Spirit rose up from within Him to be on Him. "For the one whom God has sent speaks the words of God, for God gives the Spirit without limit" (John 3:34). The title Messiah (*mashiach*) means "anointed one."

Jesus is the Head and we are His body. The anointing that is poured out over Him flows down to cover us. Look at this description of Aaron's anointing from Psalm 133:2.

It is like precious oil poured on the head,
  running down on the beard,
running down on Aaron's beard,
  down on the collar of his robe.

I pray a prayer that comes from that picture of the anointing: "Let my life be so saturated with Your Spirit that my words, actions, and thoughts drip with His presence. Pour out Your Spirit without limit."

HOLY, HOLY, HOLY

This oil was called the holy anointing oil. It was not to be used for any other purpose, and was not to be poured out on flesh (Exodus 30:30–33). It was only to be poured out on the covering (garments) that covered the priests' flesh.

The anointing of His Spirit that we receive in us is for holiness, not power. Power flows from purity, but the anointing is for producing purity in our lives. To find power, seek purity.

The anointing poured out on us produces a sweet-smelling aroma before the Lord. "For we are to God the pleasing aroma of Christ" (2 Corinthians 2:15). We are the aroma of Christ, both to the saved and to the unsaved. This picture of aroma is a particularly interesting one. I wrote about it years ago in my book *Riches Stored in Secret Places*. Let me recap.

THE POWER OF AROMA

Of all the physical senses, the sense of smell is the strongest. Aromas are imprinted indelibly on the memory. You remember everything you have ever smelled and the memory of it is activated when you smell the aroma again. Aroma will stir up a memory and all the emotions attached to it. Perhaps when you smell cinnamon, you are transported in your memory to your grandmother's kitchen and the aroma of cinnamon creates in you a sense of being warm and safe and loved. You don't necessarily bring all of this to consciousness, but you love the smell of cinnamon.

Information that the brain gathers from the other senses goes through a complex processing procedure before it reaches the thalamus, where the brain assigns emotions to it. Of course, this all happens in nano-seconds, so it seems to be immediate. Smell, on the other hand, goes directly to the thalamus. Without being processed it immediately produces an emotional reaction. Aroma has an immediate, strong, and lasting impact. Yet, because it is not processed in the same way other stimuli from the environment are processed, this impact is visceral, not necessarily recognized in the information-processing aspects of your consciousness. It is purely emotional.

Smell, when it is pleasant, draws you to its source. When you walk into a grocery store and immediately smell freshly baked bread, what happens? You begin to desire freshly baked bread. Smell stirs up something called "sensory integration." All of your senses become involved in the desiring. You imagine how freshly baked bread looks, feels, and tastes. Finally, you purchase freshly baked bread.

How interesting, then, that the Creator, who created the senses, should choose the picture of aroma to teach us how Christ is made known to the world.

Paul ties this imagery to a familiar scene for his readers: the triumphal procession. He creates a mental picture of a triumphal procession, in which a triumphant Roman general is celebrated for his victorious campaign. The conquering general is preceded into the city by the captives taken in war and is followed by his triumphant troops. As the conquering troops paraded through the city, they shout, "Triumph!"

Included in the triumphal procession were the priests of the general's gods swinging censers filled with burning incense. The streets and temple were decorated with fragrant garlands. Aroma was an important feature of the triumphal procession. When the procession reached its destination, the temple of Jupiter, the captives were led off to their execution. The aroma of the procession was a smell that denoted victory for the triumphant and death for those triumphed over. The same smell held differing meanings, depending upon one's position in the procession.

My dad grew up on a farm in Missouri. I remember as a child when we would visit a farm, my nose would be assaulted with the horrible smells of animals and hay and farm things. Just as I was be thinking, What a terrible smell!, my dad would say, "I just love these smells!" I always wondered if we were smelling the same aroma, or if grown-ups could smell things children could not.

The very same aroma was a sweet savor to my dad and an awful stench to me. The same smell had different emotional associations for each of us and those associations determined its impact. Paul tells us that the aroma of Christ is disseminated throughout the world, both to those who are in the process of being saved and to those who are in the process of dying eternally. To one it is the smell of life, to the other, it is the stench of death. It attracts the one and repels the other. His children call out, "Your name is like a perfume poured out" (Song of Solomon 1:3). Among His enemies, His name is reviled and ridiculed and defamed. Same aroma, different reactions.

ONLY JESUS SMELLS LIKE JESUS

An aroma identifies its source. A rose, for example, emits an aroma that you will immediately identify as a rose. "I smell a rose," you will say. A rose may have many different names as it is translated into different languages, but the smell identifies it as a rose. "A rose by any other name would smell as sweet," Shakespeare writes.

The aroma of Christ comes from the Spirit of Christ. The fragrance of Christ will not be produced by good works, or moral behavior, or by answering correctly, or by following the rules. Only Jesus smells like Jesus.

Paul says that the aroma of Christ is introduced into the world through you and me: "who through us spreads everywhere the fragrance of the knowledge of him." We are the censers that hold the sweet-smelling incense. Jesus' life is operating on earth in and through us. He lives in us and is expressed through us.

—ᗰ—

1. Is there any part of your life or personality that is not given access to the very Spirit of God? Is there any part of your life or personality to which you are withholding access from the Spirit? You have access to Him. Does He have access to you? Evaluate and write out your thoughts.

MIND:

Thoughts and opinions

Memories

Understanding

Wisdom

Insight

Other

EMOTIONS:

Reactions to events and circumstances

Emotions from the past that spill into the present situation

Love toward individuals

Other

WILL:

Desires and dreams

Acts of obedience

Other

2. How do you see the anointing of the Spirit on your life wafting to others?

3. Where in your life are you still operating in the power of flesh, and hoping the anointing will be there? Where do you still depend on your own strength and abilities instead of letting the anointing of the Anointed flow?

FULL SPECTRUM SALVATION

God has provided a full salvation. He did not leave us on our own to do the best we can. He has given us everything we need to walk out our freedom. The Spirit is present to empower and direct every detail of our lives. "Since we live by the Spirit, let us keep in step with the Spirit" (Galatians 5:25).

K. S. Weust says *(Wuest's Word Studies from the Greek New Testament: For the English reader)* that Paul's instruction to the Galatians meant, since they "have divine life resident in their beings, to conduct themselves under the guidance, impulses, and energy of that life."

—ɯ—

With that definition of walking out the details of your life under the guidance, impulses, and energy of the Spirit, how would you expand on the following?

Pray in the Spirit
"And pray in the Spirit on all occasions with all kinds of prayers and requests. With this in mind, be alert and always keep on praying for all the Lord's people" (Ephesians 6:118). Consider Romans 8:26–27.

Worship in the Spirit
"God is spirit, and his worshipers must worship in the Spirit and in truth" (John 4:24).

Serve in the Spirit

"For it is we who are the circumcision, we who serve God by his Spirit, who boast in Christ Jesus, and who put no confidence in the flesh" (Philippians 3:3).

ABANDONED TO HIM

The ultimate aim of being clothed with the Holy Spirit is that we become fully abandoned to the Father, through the Son, by the Spirit. We are living, breathing offerings. We are living worship. God is seeking worshippers who will worship Him in spirit and in truth. When the Anointing of the Anointed is so released in you, and then through you, that your life smells like Jesus, then you are the very definition of worship. Offering up to God all that we are. William Temple defines worship like this in *Readings in St John's Gospel*:

> *Worship is the submission of all our nature to God. It is the quickening of conscience by His holiness; the nourishment of mind with His truth; the purifying of imagination by His Beauty; the opening of the heart to His love; the surrender of will to His purpose — and all of this gathered up in adoration, the most selfless emotion of which our nature is capable and therefore the chief remedy for that self-centeredness which is our original sin and the source of all actual sin.*

The Spirit of Jesus will produce in us the character and heart of Jesus. We will find ourselves joyfully abandoned to the will of the Father. If the question is: What is my will? Then the answer is: The Father's will. We will say with Jesus:

"I have food to eat that you know nothing about." Then his disciples said to each other, "Could someone have brought him food?" "My food," said Jesus, "is to do the will of him who sent me and to finish his work (John 4:32–34).

USING CLOTHED WITH POWER

IN YOUR GROUP
— SESSION VIDEOS

VIDEO GUIDE

Your group members can use digital QR readers to see small portions of the DVD sessions at any time, using the QR links posted in this book, beginning with the code in the book introduction. At publication, several readers are available as free apps for participants to download onto portable digital devices.

However, those QR links reveal shorter-length segments (approximately 15 to 90 seconds) of the actual video sessions you'll use during group time. Each of the video sessions for use in group is approximately 10 to 15 minutes in duration. Those videos can be viewed in total—or you may choose to pause for group discussion. Whatever works best for your group is the goal.

The video sessions are designed to introduce your group to the concepts they will study during the week. These video sessions integrate directly with the content in group members' books, providing a brief overview of a week's study content and related Scripture, terms, and concepts. The video sessions help to connect and cement study content to your group members' understanding, internalization, and application.

The DVD is compatible with most DVD players, desktop and laptop computers that have the DVD playing option. The shorter QR segments are accessible on an online platform and members can use a variety of mobile devices that have a QR reader app (application).

HOW TO USE

Play the video session at the end of your study session to launch the upcoming week's material.

WEEK 1: However, at the beginning of week one session with your group, you can use the "Week 1 intro" to the study. You will need to

PAUSE or STOP the DVD after the short intro, before the white title "Week 1" appears.

Following your presentation of the intro, talk about what you want to learn from a study on the Holy Spirit's role in your life. Talk about the phrase "clothed with power" and what that phrase pictures for you in terms of the Holy Spirit in your life. Spend time in prayer for insight and understanding.

At the end of your session, then use the Week 1 video to encourage group participants as they prepare for study. At the conclusion of the Week 1 video session, the DVD will automatically return you to the DVD menu (most DVD players will skip to the next session automatically when played on fast-forward mode).

WEEK 2 THROUGH WEEK 6: During each of your sessions, let people talk about the most meaningful concept from the week's material and how that has an impact on their lives. As conversation starters during the session, use the interactive questions posed in the Bible study book as well as the QR videos as discussion starters. You can show the week's video at the end of your session to introduce the upcoming week's material. The Week 6 video session also includes a short conclusion following the main session segment.

EXTRAS

We share some explanation of some study terms mentioned, which your group may find helpful.

PROMO

At the end of the DVD, right before "Credits," you'll find an approximately 15-second promo you can use to share as an overview of the Clothed with Power opportunity — an announcement — to engage participation, enthusiasm, and to explain what members can anticipate from this study when they participate in it.

VIEWER VIDEO NOTES

WEEK ONE

WEEK TWO

WEEK THREE

WEEK FOUR

WEEK FIVE

WEEK SIX

New Hope® Publishers is a division of WMU®, an international organization that challenges Christian believers to understand and be radically involved in God's mission. For more information about WMU, go to wmu.com. More information about New Hope books may be found at NewHopeDigital.com. New Hope books may be purchased at your local bookstore.

Use the QR reader on your
smartphone to visit us online at
NewHopeDigital.com

If you've been blessed by this book, we would like to hear your story.
The publisher and author welcome your comments and
suggestions at: newhopereader@wmu.org.

Other Dynamic Studies by This Author

Life Unhindered!
Five Keys to Walking in Freedom

ISBN-13: 978-1-59669-286-2
N104143 • $14.99

Live a Praying Life!
*Open Your Life to God's
Power and Provision*

ISBN-13: 978-1-59669-299-2
N104149 • $19.99

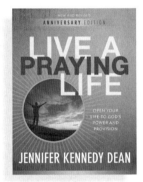

Power in the Blood
of Christ

ISBN-13: 978-1-59669-363-0
N134106 • $14.99

Set Apart
A 6-Week Study of the Beatitudes

ISBN-13: 978-1-59669-263-3
N104132 • $14.99

*Available in bookstores everywhere. For information about these books
or this author, visit NewHopeDigital.com.*

NEW HOPE
PUBLISHERS
Gospel-Centered. Missions-Driven.

Fit for HEAVEN. Designed for REDEMPTION.

As a believer you are wearing God's perfect design for you. He chooses to work like a tailor-made suit—one that is custom-fit just for the individual. His perfect fit is designed to draw attention to our best features and diminish our weaknesses. *Clothed with Power* helps you explore how the Holy Spirit is at work in every area of your life. Designed as a six-week interactive study, national best-selling author and prayer expert Jennifer Kennedy Dean uses the symbolism of the Old Testament priests' garments to show you anew how your salvation has always been a part of God's redemptive plan.

An accompanying DVD to this study is also available. Inside, see scenes from this study's accompanying DVD with your digital device.

"In a brilliant unveiling of the priestly garments, Jennifer illustrates the role of the Holy Spirit in our lives and how He clothes us with power from on high."
—GARI MEACHAM, best-selling author of *Spirit Hunger* and founder of Truly Fed Ministries

Jennifer digs deeply—but understandably—into what it means to be clothed with power, as Jesus promised we would be. I love this book!"
—EVA MARIE EVERSON, director of the Florida Christian Writers Conference

---

JENNIFER KENNEDY DEAN is executive director of the Praying Life Foundation and a respected author and speaker. She is the author of numerous books, studies, and magazine articles specializing in prayer and spiritual formation. Her book *Heart's Cry* has been named National Day of Prayer's signature book. Her book *Live a Praying Life* has been called a flagship work on prayer. Widely recognized as an unusually gifted communicator of the deep truths of God's Word, Jennifer speaks all over the country calling God's people to discover the difference between a prayer life and a praying life. Jennifer has also authored *Set Apart, Fueled by Faith, Power in the Name of Jesus, Power in the Blood of Christ,* and *Secrets Jesus Shared.* A highly demanded speaker, her engagements include respected organizations such as the Billy Graham Training Center at the Cove and Focus on the Family. She is a board member for Advanced Writers and Speakers Association, a member of America's National Prayer Committee, and a member of National Professional Women Association.

RELIGION / Biblical Studies / Biblical Study Guides

ISBN-10: 1-59669-373-8
ISBN-13: 978-1-59669-373-9

NEW HOPE
PUBLISHERS

9 781596 693739

N134114